The Weekend Estate Planning Kit

Your Complete Guide to Planning for the Future

Douglas E. Godbe
Attorney at Law

SPHINX® PUBLISHING
AN IMPRINT OF SOURCEBOOKS, INC.®
NAPERVILLE, ILLINOIS
www.SphinxLegal.com

First Edition: 2007

Published by: **Sphinx® Publishing, An Imprint of Sourcebooks, Inc.®**

Naperville Office
P.O. Box 4410
Naperville, Illinois 60567-4410
630-961-3900
Fax: 630-961-2168
www.sourcebooks.com
www.SphinxLegal.com

This publication is designed to provide accurate and authoritative information in regard to the subject matter covered. It is sold with the understanding that the publisher is not engaged in rendering legal, accounting, or other professional service. If legal advice or other expert assistance is required, the services of a competent professional person should be sought.

From a Declaration of Principles Jointly Adopted by a Committee of the American Bar Association and a Committee of Publishers and Associations

This product is not a substitute for legal advice.

Disclaimer required by Texas statutes.

Library of Congress Cataloging-in-Publication Data

Godbe, Douglas, 1951-
  The weekend estate planning kit / by Douglas E. Godbe. --
1st ed.
      p. cm.
  Includes index.
  ISBN-13: 978-1-57248-605-8 (pbk. : alk. paper)
  ISBN-10: 1-57248-605-8 (pbk. : alk. paper)
  1. Estate planning--United States--Popular works. I. Title.

KF750.Z9G625 2007
346.7305'2--dc22

                                                          2007015204

Printed and bound in the United States of America.
SB — 10 9 8 7 6 5 4 3 2 1

Contents

What is a Will?
What is a Trust?
What is Probate?
Finding the Law
Community Property
Marital Property
Quasi-Community Property
Income Taxes
Estate Taxes
Do You Need a Lawyer?

Assets Subject to Disposition by a Will
Property Subject to Disposition in a Will, but Passing without
    Probate to a Surviving Spouse

Trustee
Custodian
Conclusion of Fiduciary Positions

Will Execution
Execution of Inter Vivos Trust
Keeping Your Will Safe
Keeping Your Inter Vivos Trust Safe
Revocation

Changes before Execution
Changes after Execution

Will
Inter Vivos Trust
Conclusion

Using Self-Help Law Books

Before using a self-help law book, you should realize the advantages and disadvantages of doing your own legal work and understand the challenges and diligence that this requires.

The Growing Trend

Rest assured that you will not be the first or only person handling your own legal matter. For example, in some states, more than 75% of the people in divorces and other cases represent themselves. Because of the high cost of legal services, this is a major trend, and many courts are struggling to make it easier for people to represent themselves. However, some courts are not happy with people who do not use attorneys and refuse to help them in any way. For some, the attitude is, "Go to the law library and figure it out for yourself."

We write and publish self-help law books to give people an alternative to the often complicated and confusing legal books found in most law libraries. We have made the explanations of the law as simple and easy to understand as possible. Of course, unlike an attorney advising an individual client, we cannot cover every conceivable possibility.

Cost/Value Analysis

Whenever you shop for a product or service, you are faced with various levels of quality and price. In deciding what product or service to buy, you make a cost/value analysis on the basis of your willingness to pay and the quality you desire.

When buying a car, you decide whether you want transportation, comfort, status, or sex appeal. Accordingly, you decide among choices such as a Neon, a Lincoln, a Rolls Royce, or a Porsche. Before making a decision, you usually weigh the merits of each option against the cost.

When you get a headache, you can take a pain reliever (such as aspirin) or visit a medical specialist for a neurological examination. Given this choice, most people, of course, take a pain reliever, since it costs only pennies; whereas a medical examination costs hundreds of dollars and takes a lot of time. This is usually a logical choice because it is rare to need anything more than a pain reliever for a headache. But in some cases, a headache may indicate a brain tumor, and failing to see a specialist right away can result in complications. Should everyone with a headache go to a specialist? Of course not, but people treating their own illnesses must realize that they are betting, on the basis of their cost/value analysis of the situation, that they are taking the most logical option.

The same cost/value analysis must be made when deciding to do one's own legal work. Many legal situations are very straightforward, requiring a simple form and no complicated analysis. Anyone with a little intelligence and a book of instructions can handle the matter without outside help.

But there is always the chance that complications are involved that only an attorney would notice. To simplify the law into a book like this, several legal cases often must be condensed into a single sentence or paragraph. Otherwise, the book would be several hundred pages long and too complicated for most people. However, this simplification necessarily leaves out many details and nuances that would apply to special or unusual situations. Also, there are many ways to interpret most legal questions. Your case may come before a judge who disagrees with the analysis of our authors.

Therefore, in deciding to use a self-help law book and to do your own legal work, you must realize that you are making a cost/value analysis. You have decided that the money you will save in doing it yourself outweighs the chance that your case will not turn out to your satisfaction. Most people handling their own simple legal matters never have a problem, but occasionally people find that it ended up costing them more to have an attorney straighten out the situation than it would have if they had hired an attorney in the beginning. Keep this in mind while handling your case, and be sure to consult an attorney if you feel you might need further guidance.

Local Rules

The next thing to remember is that a book which covers the law for the entire nation, or even for an entire state, cannot possibly include every procedural difference of every jurisdiction. Whenever possible, we provide the exact form needed; however, in some areas, each county, or even each judge, may require unique forms and procedures. In our state books, our forms usually cover the majority of counties in the state or provide examples of the type of form that will be required. In our national books, our forms are sometimes even more general in nature but are designed to give a good idea of the type of form that will be needed in most locations. Nonetheless, keep in mind that your state, county, or judge may have a requirement, or use a form, that is not included in this book.

You should not necessarily expect to be able to get all of the information and resources you need solely from within the pages of this book. This book will serve as your guide, giving you specific information whenever possible and helping you to find out what else you will need to know. This is just like if you decided to build your own backyard deck. You might purchase a book on how to build decks. However, such a book would not include the building codes and permit requirements of every city, town, county, and township in the nation; nor would it include the lumber, nails, saws, hammers, and other materials and tools you would need to actually build the deck. You would use the book as your guide, and then do some work and research involving such matters as whether you need a permit of some kind, what type and grade of wood is available in your area, whether to use hand tools or power tools, and how to use those tools.

Before using the forms in a book like this, you should check with your court clerk to see if there are any local rules of which you should be aware or local forms you will need to use. Often, such forms will require the same information as the forms in the book but are merely laid out differently or use slightly different language. They will sometimes require additional information.

Changes in the Law

Besides being subject to local rules and practices, the law is subject to change at any time. The courts and the legislatures of all fifty states are constantly revising the laws. It is possible that while you are reading this book, some aspect of the law is being changed.

In most cases, the change will be of minimal significance. A form will be redesigned, additional information will be required, or a waiting period will be extended. As a result, you might need to revise a form, file an extra form, or wait out a longer time period. These types of changes will not usually affect the outcome of your case. On the other hand, sometimes a major part of the law is changed, the entire law in a particular area is rewritten, or a case that was the basis of a central legal point is overruled. In such instances, your entire ability to pursue your case may be impaired.

How to Use the CD-ROM

Thank you for purchasing *The Weekend Estate Planning Kit*. In this book, we have worked hard to compile exactly what you need to prepare all your estate planning documents. To make this material even more useful, we have included every document in the book on the CD-ROM in the back of the book.

You can use these forms just as you would the forms in the book. Print them out, fill them in, and use them however you need. You can also fill in the forms directly on your computer. Just identify the form you need, open it, click on the space where the information should go, and input your information. Customize each form for your particular needs. Use them over and over again.

The CD-ROM is compatible with both PC and Mac operating systems. (While it should work with either operating system, we cannot guarantee that it will work with your particular system and we cannot provide technical assistance.) To use the forms on your computer, you will need to use Microsoft Word or another word processing program that can read Word files. The CD-ROM does not contain any such program.

Insert the CD-ROM into your computer. Double-click on the icon representing the disc on your desktop or go through your hard drive to identify the drive that contains the disc and click on it.

Once opened, you will see the files contained on the CD-ROM listed as "Form #: [Form Title]." Open the file you need. You may print the form to fill it out manually at this point, or you can click on the appropriate line to fill it in using your computer.

Any time you see bracketed information [ ] on the form, you can click on it and delete the bracketed information from your final form. This information is only a reference guide to assist you in filling in the forms and should be removed from your final version. Once all your information is filled in, you can print your filled-in form.

*   *   *   *   *

Purchasers of this book are granted a license to use the forms contained in it for their own personal use. By purchasing this book, you have also purchased a limited license to use all forms on the accompanying CD-ROM. The license limits you to personal use only and all other copyright laws must be adhered to. No claim of copyright is made in any government form reproduced in the book or on the CD-ROM. You are free to modify the forms and tailor them to your specific situation.

The author and publisher have attempted to provide the most current and up-to-date information available. However, the courts, Congress, and your state's legislatures review, modify, and change laws on an ongoing basis, as well as create new laws from time to time. Due to the very nature of the information and the continual changes in our legal system, to be sure that you have the current and best information for your situation, you should consult a local attorney or research the current laws yourself.

Introduction

Estate planning is an essential activity for every individual and couple. It can protect your assets, provide for minor children, and potentially save millions of dollars in taxes. Careful planning can provide peace of mind and ensure maximum wealth transfer at your death. This book can serve as a guide to begin your estate planning, as it contains basic forms that most people can use to accomplish their goals.

The purpose of this book is to:

- describe basic law regarding the disposition of assets by will, by a living trust (called an *inter vivos trust*), by joint tenancy, and by transfer on death (TOD) methods (such as Totten trusts, pension plan beneficiary designations, and life insurance beneficiary designations);
- guide you through the preparation and execution of a will, a codicil to a will, an inter vivos trust (and the funding of the inter vivos trust), an amendment to an inter vivos trust, and nomination of guardian without a lawyer;
- advise when you need a lawyer;
- describe the types of property that pass at death without a will or inter vivos trust; and,
- provide over fifty different blank forms for wills, inter vivos trusts, codicils, amendments to inter vivos trusts, nominations of guardians, and so on, as well as samples of completed forms for wills, inter vivos trusts, and nominations of guardians to fit most family situations and estate disposition objectives.

Reading the book and following the instructions will enable you to prepare (using the fill-in-the-blank forms found on the accompanying CD-ROM) and execute a will, an inter vivos trust, and a nomination of guardian. This book also warns you of situations when you need to hire an attorney. After reviewing this book, you might decide to consult with an attorney either to draft your estate plan or to review the will or inter vivos trust you have prepared from the forms included in this book. In that event, this book will help you determine what your estate planning objectives are and better understand the process when guided by your attorney.

Some estate planners call a will the *wastebasket of estate planning* because, contrary to popular belief, very few assets are disposed of at death under a will. This book identifies types of property ownership titles that avoid both disposition under a will and probate through the court.

This book explains why the inter vivos trust has become so popular in the last twenty years. It gives you the information you need to determine if the inter vivos trust is appropriate for your situation and estate.

The differences between making outright bequests, leaving someone a life estate in an asset, using custodianships for minors, and using trusts to manage and distribute assets for a beneficiary are explained. This legal kit will discuss federal estate taxes, state inheritance taxes, and how to plan your estate to minimize or even completely avoid those death taxes.

Twenty-four different wills, two nominations of guardians, ten inter vivos trusts, and more than fifteen other forms are provided for your use. Sample, filled-in forms and step-by-step forms with instructions are provided to assist you in completing the forms for yourself. The will and inter vivos trust forms included with this book cover four basic family situations: married with children, married without children, unmarried with children, and unmarried without children. Separate forms are provided for the nomination of guardians for minor children.

An asset roadmap form is also provided. It will help you identify assets—both for your own estate planning decisions and to assist the person you appoint to manage your estate after your death. You can use the forms directly from the book, photocopy them, or use the blank versions found on the accompanying CD-ROM.

This book does not cover the subjects of generation-skipping transfers limitations, qualified charitable unitrusts, or remainder trusts.

Chapter 1 is a general section that will familiarize you with various terms and concepts in planning your will or inter vivos trust. It also covers estate and inheritance taxes. Chapter 2 explains the types of assets that are subject to disposition under a will and which assets can be distributed at death without a will. Chapter 3 discusses some of the differences in estate planning choices and the advantages and disadvantages of those choices to assist you in coordinating your estate plan.

Chapter 4 discusses who can be listed as beneficiaries, and as such, who can inherit. Issues related to adult beneficiaries versus beneficiaries who are still minors and persons who may be disqualified to inherit due to relationship to the testator are also discussed. Chapter 5 discusses the various types of bequests that can be made. It discusses the advantages and disadvantages of outright bequests, bequests for the lifetime use of the beneficiary (life estates), bequests to minors (custodianships and trusts instead of guardianships), and bequests in trust for a beneficiary's lifetime. Chapter 6 discusses how to select an executor to probate your will. It also explains how to select a trustee to administer your inter vivos trust or a trust created under your will, and how to select a guardian to care for your orphaned children.

Chapter 1:

An Overview

Before preparing your will or drafting your trust, it is helpful to review some of the fundamentals of estate planning and ask yourself a couple of questions. This chapter will explore the basics of what the key documents are and assist you in determining which is best for you.

What is a Will?

A *will* is a written document that disposes of a person's property at the death of that person. To be valid, a will must be signed by the person, called the *testator*, whose property it affects.

What is a Trust?

The term *trust* refers to an arrangement where one person holds legal title to property for the benefit of another person. For example, say Bob holds title to 1,000 shares of IBM stock, as trustee for Mary. The written trust document provides that trust income is paid to Mary, so Bob would pay the IBM stock dividends to Mary.

There are many kinds of trusts for many different reasons. However, the trust that is often used as a will substitute is generally called a *grantor trust, revocable trust, living trust,* or *inter vivos trust.* This book will refer to such a trust as an *inter vivos trust.* An inter vivos trust permits property to be distributed at death without the requirement of *probate.* A trust can also be created after death in a person's will. This type of trust is called a *testamentary trust.*

What is Probate?

Probate is the court supervision of the distribution of the *assets* of a deceased person to his or her *beneficiaries* or *heirs.* Probate exists because there is no other way to change the title to assets from the deceased person's name to the persons entitled under a will, or to the heirs by *intestate succession* if there is no will.

Assets Not Probated

As a simple guideline, all assets of the decedent must go through probate unless the law specifically provides otherwise. However, most property that belonged to a deceased person does not go through probate, because there are numerous exceptions to probate. Assets that do not pass through probate include:

- ◆ assets in which the ownership title lists the decedent and at least one living person as *joint tenants;*
- ◆ assets passing outright to a surviving spouse (this is only true in some states and does not include property passing by will to a trust for the benefit of a surviving spouse);
- ◆ bank accounts in which the ownership title is in the decedent's name as *trustee for* or *in trust for* a living person (a Totten trust);
- ◆ brokerage accounts in which the ownership title is in the decedent's name with the designation *transfer on death* to one or more living persons;
- ◆ bank accounts or savings bonds in which the ownership title is in the name of the decedent with the instruction to pay on death to one or more living persons;
- ◆ assets in which the ownership title is in the name of the trustee of an inter vivos trust;
- ◆ assets belonging to the decedent wherein the decedent, by contract, designated at least one beneficiary or payee in the event of death (such as pension plans, IRAs, 401(k) plans, or life insurance), and the beneficiary survived the decedent; and,

◆ assets in which the ownership title is in the name of the decedent, but the assets have a small gross value (the actual amount varies from state to state).

NOTE: *A decedent often leaves both assets that can be transferred at his or her death without probate and assets that must be transferred via a probate process.*

Finding the Law

The law itself is found primarily in the *Probate Code* for each state. Each state's Probate Code can be purchased in most law bookstores for about $25, and these laws are also generally available on several Internet websites. A good way to find the statutes in your state is to use a search engine and type in the name of your state's code as found in Appendix A (i.e., "Arizona Revised Statutes Annotated + probate").

Community Property

In Arizona, California, Idaho, Louisiana, Nevada, New Mexico, Texas, Washington, and Wisconsin property is either separate property or community property.

Separate property describes the assets of a single, divorced, or widowed person, or the assets of a married person that were acquired before marriage or during marriage by gift or inheritance.

Although the laws differ from state to state, *community property* is generally defined as property acquired during marriage by a married person, unless acquired by gift or inheritance.

In most community property states, the income from separate property is also separate property, but this can be modified depending on the time and effort expended by one or both of the spouses in maintaining the property.

Example: *Helen, at the time of marriage, owns a successful retail store. During her marriage to Jason, she expends considerable time and expertise on the business, takes a very small salary, puts most of the profits back into the business, and expands to a chain of one hundred retail stores. At her death, Helen's business might be considered partly community property, as her efforts were put back into the business.*

Further, in community property states, the separate property of one spouse can be commingled with community property to the extent that the separate property is no longer traceable and becomes community property.

NOTE: *In some community property states, community property may be held in the name of only one of the spouses.*

Another aspect of community property is that each spouse may generally transfer, at his or her death, his or her one-half interest in any community property asset to someone other than the *surviving spouse*. The surviving spouse's one-half interest in the community property, regardless of the disposition made by the predeceased spouse, is not affected by the predeceased spouse's disposition of his or her one-half interest in the community property.

Community property can only exist during the marriage. At the moment of the death of either spouse, the property becomes separate property—one-half owned by the deceased spouse and one-half owned by the surviving spouse. Any property inherited from the deceased spouse by the surviving spouse becomes the separate property of the surviving spouse.

Marital Property

In non-community property states, property acquired during the marriage is generally referred to as *marital property*. While the distinction between community property and separate property is important, community property and marital property are essentially the same. (This book will use the term *community property* throughout when referring to property acquired during the marriage, with each spouse owning a one-half interest.)

Quasi-Community Property

Quasi-community property is recognized in a few community property states, such as California. It is property acquired by a married person who dies a resident of the community property state, while owning property acquired while he or she was living outside of the community property state. At the time of death, that property must have been considered community property if the person had been living in the community property state at the time the property was acquired. In such a situation, the quasi-community property is treated like community property.

Income Taxes

Taxes are an issue whether or not a decedent's estate goes through probate. For estate planning purposes, there are three tax issues to be concerned with— income taxes to the beneficiaries on bequests, the income tax basis adjustments as a result of the decedent's death, and estate and inheritance taxes.

Income Taxation of Inheritance

What a beneficiary receives from an estate is *not* generally subject to income taxes, with some exceptions.

Example: *You leave your nephew a $50,000 bequest in your will. The $50,000 check your nephew receives from your estate after your death is not subject to income tax on his personal income tax return.*

One of the common exceptions would be retirement plan payments, such as IRAs. They are taxable as income to the beneficiary who receives plan proceeds.

Income Tax Basis Adjustment

If you buy ABC Corp. stock for $10 per share and then sell it for $25 per share, you have a $15 per share profit called a *capital gain*. If you sell your ABC Corp. stock for $2 a share, you have an $8 per share loss called a *capital loss*. In either situation, your purchase cost of $10 per share is your *basis* for income tax purposes. Capital gains are subject to income taxation.

For federal income tax purposes, at the decedent's death, his or her assets receive a new income tax basis, regardless of the original cost basis. The new basis is the value of the asset as of the date of death. (Internal Revenue Code (I.R.C.) 1014.) If the decedent's assets increase in value from his or her date of acquisition to his or her date of death, this new basis is an income tax advantage to the estate or the beneficiary of the estate who inherits the property. Obviously, if the decedent's assets decrease in value from date of acquisition to date of death, the new basis is an income tax disadvantage to the estate or the beneficiary of the estate who inherits the property.

Generally, state income tax law provides the same date of death *basis adjustment* as does federal income tax law.

Double basis adjustment for community property. Under federal income tax law, community property held by a decedent and his or her spouse receives a basis adjustment at the decedent's death on both the decedent's one-half interest in the community property and on the surviving spouse's one-half interest, unless the property was held in joint tenancy. (The property can be held in one spouse's name or both spouses' names, but just not in joint tenancy.) (I.R.C. 1014(b)(6).)

Example 1: *Bill and Sue, husband and wife, buy rental property for $100,000 using community property funds, and hold title in Bill's name only. Sue dies four years later. At her death, the property is worth $300,000. The new income tax basis of the property is stepped up to Sue's date of death value of $300,000. The new basis value would be used to restart depreciation or measure capital gain or loss in the event of eventual sale.*

Example 2: *Consider the same facts as in Example 1, except that title is held in the name of husband and wife as joint tenants. At Sue's death, the new income basis would be (assuming no prior depreciation) $200,000. (Sue's one-half interest would receive a basis adjustment step up from $50,000 to $150,000, and Bill's one-half interest would remain at $50,000, for a total of $200,000).*

On the other hand, if husband and wife have a community property asset (not held in joint tenancy) that goes down in value, then a double step down in the income tax basis would occur. Therefore, from an income tax standpoint, a husband and wife should not hold title to community property that appreciated in value in joint tenancy, and should hold title to community property that has depreciated in value in joint tenancy.

Income tax basis exceptions. Some types of properties for which the decedent had not paid income taxes do not receive the basis adjustment at date of death. IRAs, pension plans, installment sales notes, and savings bonds do not receive a basis adjustment equal to the date of death value.

Estate Taxes

The federal government imposes a tax upon estates called the *estate tax*. The estate tax applies to all of the decedent's property, whether it goes through probate or passes by contract (IRAs, pension plans, annuities, life insurance), via an inter vivos trust, by survivorship (joint tenancy, Totten trust, payable on death accounts), or by operation of law (property passing to a surviving spouse). A common misconception is that if the decedent's estate avoids probate, then it avoids the federal estate tax.

In addition to applying to all property in which the decedent had an interest at time of death, the federal estate tax also applies to all gifts made by the decedent during his or her lifetime that exceeded the annual exclusion amount for gifts. All gifts in excess of $12,000 made by the decedent to any one donee in any calendar year are *added* to the decedent's date of death assets to compute the federal estate tax.

Example: *If Ralph, in 2005, gave Bob Smith $13,000 and Mary Jones $9,000, then the $1,000 excess gift to Bob would be added to Ralph's estate at time of his death for purposes of computing the federal estate tax. The first $12,000 of Bob's gift is not included, and neither is any of the gift to Mary, as said gift was under $12,000.*

Even some property that the decedent did not own can be included in his or her estate for purposes of computing the federal estate tax. For example, life insurance policy proceeds from a policy on the life of the decedent that are given away by the decedent within three years of the decedent's death are wholly included in the decedent's estate. Also included are assets that the decedent gave away, but from which he or she retained the right to receive income.

Example: *Raj gives away his IBM stock during his lifetime, but retains the right to receive the dividends on the gifted IBM stock. In that event, the full value of the IBM stock is included in Raj's estate for purposes of computing the federal estate tax.*

Furthermore, assets in which the decedent was a joint tenant are presumed to wholly belong to the decedent (unless the joint tenancy is held with the decedent's spouse, in which case the presumption is that one-half of the joint tenancy belonged to the decedent).

The good news is that 98% of decedents' estates never pay any federal estate taxes due to various deductions and exemptions permitted by law. The decedent's estate is permitted to deduct the value of assets passing to a surviving spouse, whether the inheritance is outright (i.e., no strings attached) or in a *Qualified Terminable Interest Trust* (QTIP trust)—as long as the surviving spouse is a U.S. citizen—or in a *Qualified Domestic Trust* (QDOT trust) if the surviving spouse is not a U.S. citizen. Also deductible are bequests to qualified charities. The decedent's estate can also deduct all debts of the decedent at time of death including unpaid income taxes, property taxes, mortgages, reasonable funeral expenses (the IRS permits funerals that cost $20,000 and upwards, so long as the monies are actually expended), and actual costs of administering the decedent's estate (such as attorney fees, executor commissions, court costs, accountant fees, and appraisal costs). In addition, every decedents estate is given an exemption amount against the federal estate tax. For decedents dying in 2007, the exemption amount is $2,000,000. This means that unless a decedent's net estate (gross value of the estate less deductions for gifts to spouse, gifts to charity, debts at date of death, funeral expenses, and costs of estate administration) is over $2,000,000, there is no federal estate tax due. The exemption amount has scheduled increases through 2010, when the exemption amount will be unlimited—meaning no federal estate taxes regardless of the size of the estate. However, in 2011, the federal estate tax returns with a reduced exemption amount of $1,000,000, unless Congress takes further action.

Accordingly, so long as a married decedent leaves no more than the federal estate tax exemption amount to noncharitable entities or persons other than his or her spouse, there will be no federal estate taxes when that decedent dies. The decedent can be worth $100 billion, and if he or she has a will that simply states, "All to my spouse," there will be no federal estate taxes, as long as the surviving spouse is a U.S. citizen. (If the surviving spouse is not a U.S. citizen, the deduction for a bequest to a surviving spouse must be made via a Qualified Domestic Trust.) Of course, even a non-U.S. citizen surviving spouse can inherit, without federal estate taxes, up to the exemption amount from the decedent.

COMPUTING A DECEDENT'S FEDERAL ESTATE TAX

Assumption: Decedent unmarried at time of death.

Assets Included in Decedent's Estate:

Assets in decedent's estate at date of death (5/1/07):	$3,900,000
Life insurance proceeds paid on decedent's life:	125,000
Decedent's joint tenancies:	30,000
Decedent's IRA:	10,000
Excess gifts made by decedent during lifetime:	<u>25,000</u>
Total Estate Subject to Federal Estate Tax:	*$4,090,000*

Deductions:

Gifts to charity:	$100,000
Mortgages (date of death principal amount plus accrued interest):	225,000
Unpaid property taxes:	6,000
Debts (including credit cards, utility bills, medical expenses, unpaid income taxes):	7,000
Expenses of administration (attorney's fee, accountant's fee, executor's fee, appraisal fees):	10,000
Funeral expenses:	<u>12,000</u>
Total Deductions:	*$360,000*

Net Estate:	$3,730,000
Federal Estate Tax Exemption (for 2007):	<u>$2,000,000</u>
Estate subject to Federal Estate Taxes:	$1,730,000
Amount of Federal Estate Taxes (45% of $1,730,000):	$778,500

Several points to remember about the federal estate tax include the following.

◆ Nothing passing outright to a U.S. citizen surviving spouse is subject to federal estate taxes. A decedent could leave $1 billion outright to a U.S. citizen surviving spouse free of any federal estate taxes.

◆ Nothing passing to a qualified charity is subject to federal estate taxes. Besides outright bequests to charities, there are certain types of trusts wherein the charity's interest in that trust is not subject to federal estate taxes (i.e., charitable annuity trusts and charitable unitrusts).

◆ Property passing into certain types of trusts for the benefit of a surviving spouse are not subject to *immediate* federal estate taxes. Common names of trusts for a surviving spouse that *defer* the federal estate tax until the death of the surviving spouse are *marital trust, QTIP trust, QDOT trust,* and *marital deduction trust*. These types of trusts are generally created to hold assets of a decedent's estate that are in *excess* of the federal estate tax exemption amount and that the decedent did not want to give *outright* to the surviving spouse.

Example: *Jane's separate property estate is $3,000,000 when she dies in 2007. Jane could give her husband, Jack, all of her estate outright with no federal estate tax. However, Jane is concerned that Jack will, if he inherits the $3,000,000 outright, eventually leave it all to his children from a prior marriage (who Jane dislikes), and Jane wants the $3,000,000 to eventually pass to her own children from a prior marriage. Jane could leave $2,000,000 of her estate in a trust for the lifetime benefit of Jack and have that trust eventually pass to her children with no federal estate taxes, as the federal estate tax exemption in year 2007 is $2,000,000. However, what does Jane do with her remaining $1,000,000? One solution would be for Jane to leave the remaining $1,000,000 in a Qualified Terminable Interest Trust (QTIP trust) if Jack is a U.S. citizen, or in a Qualified Domestic Trust (QDOT trust) if Jack is not a U.S. citizen. Both a QTIP and a QDOT trust* *would be for the lifetime benefit of Jack, and both would permit the federal estate tax on the $1,000,000 to be deferred until the subsequent death of Jack, at which time the trust assets could go to Jane's children. In fact, to the extent Jack's estate does not fully utilize the federal estate tax exemption in the year of his subsequent death, the QTIP or QDOT trust assets could use the remainder of Jack's federal estate tax exemption.*

◆ Every decedent is entitled to a federal estate tax exemption amount. Said exemption, for decedents who die in 2007, is $2,000,000. (There are scheduled increases in the exemption through 2010, at which time the federal estate tax exemption will have no limit. In 2011, the exemption amount will revert to $1,000,000.) With proper planning, a husband and wife who both die before 2010 could leave at least $4,000,000 federal-estate-tax-free to their children, and a husband and wife who both die after 2010 could leave at least $2,000,000 federal estate tax free to their children.

◆ The federal estate tax is due nine months after the death of the decedent. Extensions to pay the federal estate tax for good cause can be granted. However, interest will be charged on the federal estate tax not paid nine months after the death of the decedent.

◆ Although the federal estate tax exemptions are significant, the federal estate tax rate starts and ends at basically 45%.

A federal estate tax return (called Form 706) must be filed if the gross value of the estate (value before deductions such as debts, mortgages, amounts passing to spouse or charity are deducted) exceeds the federal estate tax exemption in the year of the decedent's death.

Example: *If Pedro dies in 2007 owning $2,100,000 in assets and $200,000 in debts, mortgages, and other deductions, a federal estate tax return would have to be filed, as the gross value of Pedro's estate exceeded $2,000,000. However, no federal estate taxes would be due, as the net value of Pedro's estate was less than $2,000,000.*

The preparation of a federal estate tax return is best left to an attorney or certified public accountant (CPA) who specializes in preparing said returns. If a federal estate tax return is due, it must be filed before a probate estate can be closed.

Inheritance Taxes

Until 2005, there was a move away from state death taxes, generally called *inheritance taxes*. Most states were content to take a share, with the permission of the federal government, of the federal estate tax, called a *pick-up tax*. The pick-up tax collected by the state did not cost the tax-paying estate any additional federal estate taxes, as the state was literally given a portion of the federal estate tax. However, starting in 2005, the federal government stopped sharing the federal estate tax with the states. With that source of revenue gone, more and more states are enacting new inheritance taxes. Currently, the following states have some sort of inheritance tax: Connecticut, Kansas, Illinois, Indiana, Iowa, Kentucky, Maine, Massachusetts, Maryland, Minnesota, Nebraska, New Jersey, New York, North Carolina, Oklahoma, Ohio, Oregon, Pennsylvania, Rhode Island, Tennessee, Vermont, Washington, Virginia, and Wisconsin.

Generation-Skipping Taxes

If you are a wealthy individual, you might consider leaving property to your grandchildren or great-grandchildren instead of your children to avoid having that property be subject to federal estate taxes in the estate of your child when he or she dies after you. However, the federal government does not want its taxpayers avoiding the federal estate tax by *skipping* a generation and leaving property to grandchildren instead of children. Accordingly, the federal government imposes a severe tax on *generation-skipping transfers* in excess of $2,000,000 per taxpayer (for years 2006 through 2009). There are several things to consider about generation-skipping transfers. First, it is not a generation-skipping transfer to a relative if the intervening relative is deceased. For example, if your son predeceases you and you leave $4,000,000 to his son (your grandson), there is no generation-skipping transfer. Second, a transfer to a nonrelative who is more than 37.5 years younger than you is considered to be a generation-skipping transfer. The bottom line is, consult with an attorney if you are contemplating a generation skipping transfer in excess of $1,000,000 (the generation-skipping transfer limit in year 2011).

Final Note on Estate Taxes

The vast majority of decedents' deaths result in a significant tax advantage to the beneficiaries of the estate. The federal estate tax exemptions and permitted deductions to an estate means that most estates pay no federal estate taxes at all, while most estates contain appreciated assets that receive a free income tax basis step-up at time of death. You should know that the federal estate tax has been a political football for the last few years. Depending on the health of the economy and who controls Congress over the next few years, the federal estate tax laws may change substantially.

Do You Need a Lawyer?

You can, of course, hire a lawyer to provide estate tax planning advice and prepare the estate planning documents, such as a will or inter vivos trust. If this is your preference, this book will help you follow what the lawyer is doing and intelligently communicate your desires.

Beware of solicitations from nonlawyers who wish to sell a product, such as an *annuity*, in conjunction with estate planning services, such as an inter vivos trust. Usually, their main goal is the sales commission that goes with the product sale, not the achievement of an appropriate estate plan for you.

It is strongly recommended that you hire a lawyer in the following circumstances.

- ◆ The will or inter vivos trust is likely to be contested (i.e., if you believe that someone may attack the will or any of its provisions after the death of the testator or settlor).
- ◆ The testator's or settlor's estate exceeds $1,000,000. (Although the forms contained in this book are appropriate for an estate of that size or larger, it makes sense to consult with an attorney to review other estate planning options that are beyond the scope of this book.)
- ◆ The testator's or settlor's assets are complicated, such as a sole proprietorship or partnership business interest. (Again, although the forms contained in this book are appropriate for persons who own business interests, it simply makes sense to discuss those issues with an attorney and to review estate planning options that are outside the scope of this book.)

◆ The testator or settlor wishes to leave property to a disqualified person, such as a caregiver or other person who has a fiduciary relationship with the testator or settlor. (See Chapter 4 for a discussion of disqualified persons.)

◆ There are questions about the mental capacity of the testator to sign his or her will, or the capacity of the settlor to execute his or her inter vivos trust.

Many states certify lawyers as specialists in estate planning. Your state bar association or local county bar association can give you a list of the certified specialists in your area. A lawyer becomes a certified specialist by proof of experience in the area of certification and passing a test. It is no secret that lawyers who are knowledgeable in one area of the law may not know much about another area, so it makes sense to get a specialist.

If your state does not certify a specialist, the bar associations can still be of assistance in finding appropriate counsel. As with the choice of anyone you hire, a personal interview, references, costs, and a general feeling of being comfortable with the person should be your guidelines.

Chapter 2:

Assets

Not all property that a person owns is actually subject to disposition at their death by a will. This chapter discusses which assets are disposed of at death via a will and which assets are disposed of at death outside of the will—regardless of the terms of the will. There is a common misconception that all of a person's assets are disposed of by his or her will. In fact, most property passes title at death outside a will—regardless of the provisions in a will.

Assets Subject to Disposition by a Will

Assets that can be disposed of by a will include the following:

- ◆ property held in the name of the *decedent only* without any designation on the title of the asset, such as *TOD* (transfer on death), *POD* (payable on death), or as *Trustee* (trust);

– Warning –

If the decedent is married and the property in his or her name only is community property, then the decedent can only dispose of his or her one-half interest in that property. Simply because only one spouse is listed on the title does not necessarily mean that asset is separate property.

Example: *Property with the written title of "Bob" or "Bob, a single man," is an example of property held in the name of one person only.*

◆ property held by one person, another without any designation on the title, or *as tenants in common*;

Example 1: *Property has the written title of "Bob and Mary." In that event, as no type of title is indicated, the law presumes that Bob and Mary are tenants in common, meaning that each owns a separate property interest in the property.*

Example 2: *Property has the written title of "Bob and Mary, as tenants in common." Bob and Mary are tenants in common, meaning that each owns a separate property interest in the property.*

NOTE: *If a value is not specifically given to the separate property interest (e.g., a 25% interest), then the law presumes that the property is owned equally be both parties—50% each.*

◆ property held by a person and his or her spouse as *husband and wife*, or as *community property* (in this situation, each spouse can dispose of only his or her one-half community property interest by will); and,
◆ one-half of property held in the name of the person's spouse if that property is community property.

Example: *Property has the written title of "Mary." The property is community property of Mary and her spouse, Bob. Bob can, by his will, dispose of his one-half community property interest.*

Property Subject to Disposition in a Will, but Passing without Probate to a Surviving Spouse

In some states, any property left *outright* to a surviving spouse, either by will or by interstate succession, passes *without* probate. The estate could be $10,000,000, and if the deceased spouse's will says "all to my spouse," there is no probate in those states. However, if there are any restrictions on the use of the property passing to the surviving spouse (i.e., a bequest to a spouse "in trust" or to a "spouse for her lifetime use"), then the property is not passing *outright* to the surviving spouse, and the property is subject to probate.

NOTE: *Remember, the community property interest of a surviving spouse does not pass to the surviving spouse as a result of the death of the predeceasing spouse, as the surviving spouse owned it all along.*

Small Estate Distribution

Many states permit *small estates* to distribute without formal probate. While states define this term differently, a small estate is generally an estate valued under a certain amount of money. For example, in California, a small estate is under $100,000 after you subtract all joint tenancies, tenancies by the entirety, property passing by contract, PODs, TODs, Totten trusts, and property passing without probate to a surviving spouse that otherwise would go through probate, but may pass and be distributed to the beneficiary or heir without a formal probate in court.

Small estate distribution procedures are designed to be much simpler and quicker than a complete probate. They are also intended to be a less costly way to change titles to assets and pass the property of a decedent to the intended recipients.

Assets Not Subject to Disposition by a Will and Passing without Probate

Most property passes title at death without a will (or regardless of the provisions of a will) and without probate. Even when there is a probate proceeding, much of the decedent's estate will pass outside of the probate process. The reason the property described in this chapter passes without a will is due to the type of *title* that the property was held in before the death of a person, or due to a contract covering the distribution of the property on the death of the decedent.

Example: *Property that has the written title of "Bob and Mary, as joint tenants" is vested in Bob and Mary as joint tenants.*

Joint Tenancy

Joint tenancy may be the most common way that title to property passes at death without the need of a will and without the need of probate. Property can be held in the names of two or more persons as joint tenants.

Most states require that title to joint tenancy property be in writing. Sometimes the initials "JTWROS," *joint tenants with right of survivorship*, are used to designate joint tenancy property.

Example: *Property with a written title "Bob and Mary, as joint tenants" or "Bob and Mary, husband and wife, JTWROS" is joint tenancy property. Property with a written title "Bob and Mary as husband and wife" or "Bob and Mary as tenants in common" is not joint tenancy property.*

Title to joint tenancy property at the death of one of the joint tenants passes to the surviving joint tenant(s). Accordingly, all the surviving joint tenant has to do to acquire the decedent joint tenant's interest is survive the deceased joint tenant.

– Warning –

Community property held in joint tenancy between a deceased spouse and someone other than the surviving spouse is, at the death of the deceased spouse, subject to the community property interest claim of the surviving spouse. The deceased spouse did not have the right to dispose of the surviving spouse's community property interest in the joint tenancy property. In this event, contact a lawyer.

NOTE: *Property held in joint tenancy is equally owned by each joint tenant. If a father deeds his residence to himself and his child as joint tenants, the child becomes a one-half owner of the property. Even if the father is still living, the creditors of that child could attach the residence, or the child could demand the residence be sold and the proceeds equally divided. In addition, most transfers into joint tenancy are considered gifts for federal gift tax purposes, except when the asset is a bank account or the joint tenants are spouses.*

Right of Survivorship

Some states permit real estate to be held in the names of two or more persons with *right of survivorship*. This is essentially a joint tenancy without using the words "joint tenants." In such a case, the surviving owner becomes the sole owner of the real estate without probate and outside the provisions of the other owner's will.

Beneficiary Deeds

Some states permit real estate to be held in a *revocable deed,* wherein the owner of the property names a beneficiary to inherit the property at death without the need of probate and outside the provisions of the owner's will.

Tenancy by the Entirety

Tenancy by the entirety is a title used in some states as a method of holding title between spouses. Tenancy by the entirety is like joint tenancy, in that title to property passes at death without the need of a will and without the need of probate.

Example: *Property with a written title "Bob and Mary, by tenancy by the entirety" passes at death without the need of a will and probate.*

The title to property held in tenancy by the entirety passes at the death of one of the spouses to the surviving spouse. Accordingly, all the surviving spouse has to do to acquire the decedent spouse's interest is survive the predeceasing spouse.

POD and TOD Accounts

Most states permit *payable on death* (POD) and *transfer on death* (TOD) bank or brokerage accounts that transfer title at the death of the owner of the account without a will (and regardless of the provisions of the will). Of course, the accounts must be held in the name of the owner with the designation "payable on death" or "transfer on death." The difference between joint tenancy and a POD or TOD account is that the beneficiary of the POD or TOD account has no rights to the property until the death of the owner. A joint tenant is, legally, an equal co-owner of the property before the death of the other joint tenant.

– Warning –

If someone other than the surviving spouse is the named beneficiary of a POD or TOD account, the surviving spouse has a claim for his or her community property interest in the account, if the account was community property. In this event, contact a lawyer.

Contractual Accounts

Life insurance, annuities, pensions, individual retirement accounts (IRAs), and private retirement accounts are all examples of property that passes at death based upon a contract and not pursuant to the provisions in a will. The owner of the contract (the insured, the annuitant, the owner, or the employee) in essence *contracts* with the insurer, employer, or plan administrator to pay the benefits, property, or proceeds to a beneficiary designated as the recipient in the event of his or her death.

In the event the insured, annuitant, employee, or owner of the property fails to designate a beneficiary, some contracts will designate a *default* beneficiary, such as the spouse or children. At the death of the insured, annuitant, owner, or employee, the beneficiary need only execute the appropriate claim forms and submit a certified copy of the decedent's death certificate to claim the benefits, property, or proceeds.

– Warning –

If the contractual property benefits are community property or the premiums that paid for the benefits were community property, and someone other than the surviving spouse is the named beneficiary of the benefits or property, then the surviving spouse has a claim for his or her community property interest in the benefits or property. In that event, contact a lawyer.

Totten Trust Accounts

In many states, a financial institution account can be held in the name of an individual *as trustee for* or *in trust for* a named beneficiary. In this situation, the *trustee* (who is legally the owner of the account) has created a mini revocable trust for the account, commonly called a *Totten trust*. In the event of the death of the account owner, the named beneficiary becomes the owner of the account without the need of probate.

If the account is held in the name of two persons as joint tenants *as trustees for* or *in trust for* a named beneficiary, and one of the account owners dies, the surviving account owner, as the surviving joint tenant, owns all of the account, and can revoke the account or change the named beneficiary.

– Warning –

If the Totten trust account contains community property and someone other than the surviving spouse of the account holder is the named beneficiary, the surviving spouse of the account holder has a claim for his or her community property interest in the account. In this event, contact a lawyer.

Property titled in the name of an inter vivos trust, or property in a living trust with the *settlor* (the person who created and transferred the property to the trust) and the *trustee* (the one who administers and manages the trust property) being the same person, is not subject to probate. The title to property in a living trust might read something like, "John Smith, Trustee of the Smith Family Trust, dated 4/2/03."

One of the main purposes of creating a living trust is to avoid probate. Upon the death of the settlor, the trustee (often a successor trustee, as the settlor is usually the trustee until he or she dies) administers and distributes the living trust estate pursuant to the written instructions in the living trust document. The will of the settlor cannot dispose of the property held by the trust, as title to the property in the trust is held by the trust.

Inter Vivos Trust

In some states, if the settlor declares in his or her inter vivos trust that certain property is part of the trust, but fails to actually change the title of the property to the name of the inter vivos trust, a simple action can be brought in the probate court to have such property declared to be part of the trust. In this event, a lawyer should be consulted.

Chapter 3:

Deciding Which Plan Best Meets Your Goals

There is no one size fits all situation in planning your estate. A blanket statement that an inter vivos trust is the answer to all situations is just as ridiculous as a statement that a will is the best solution in all cases. You need to weigh many different factors in deciding how to structure your estate plan. In addition, you need to realize that nearly all estates are passed at death in several different ways, such as by joint tenancy, will, contract, and so on. It is important to understand and coordinate your total estate plan.

Coordinating Your Estate Plan

Before preparing a will or inter vivos trust, it is a good idea, using the ASSET ROADMAP in Appendix B of this book, to list your assets and the manner that you hold title to the assets. Remember that assets held in joint tenancy, tenancy by the entirety, TOD accounts, POD accounts, Totten trusts, inter vivos trusts, pension plans, IRAs, 401(k)s, life insurance, and annuities will pass to your intended beneficiary at death without a will and without probate. Knowing what your assets are and how they are titled might affect your decision to create a will or inter vivos trust, or the terms of either. Further, you may also decide to change the title to assets you own in your name alone to some other method that will permit transfer at your death without a will and without probate.

Example: *Rather than holding your brokerage account in the name of "Bob," have the brokerage firm change the title to "Bob, Transfer on Death to Mary." That way, Mary would receive the assets at your death without probate and regardless of any contrary provisions in your will.*

– Warning –

Creating a joint tenancy title is not recommended for property that you own in your name only, as the other joint tenant becomes a one-half owner of the property during your lifetime.

In fact, if your assets are relatively simple, you might be able to develop a plan that passes all of your estate at your death without the need of a will or inter vivos trust.

Example: *Bob's estate consists of a stock brokerage account, his 401(k) pension plan, and $200,000 in life insurance. Bob wants to leave all of his estate to his two adult daughters, Ellen and Sue. Bob could avoid probate, and the necessity of a will or inter vivos trust, simply by changing the title to his brokerage account to "Bob, TOD (transfer on death) to Ellen and Sue," and naming Ellen and Sue as the beneficiaries on his 401(k) pension plan and life insurance.*

You may, after considering all of your assets, conclude that you are going to utilize joint tenancy, contractual beneficiary designations, and an inter vivos trust or a will to have what is referred to as a *blended estate plan.*

A will allows you to direct the disposition of property you own that does not pass by joint tenancy, contract, or inter vivos trust. The advantage of a will over an inter vivos trust is that a will is a relatively simple document that can be signed and put into a safe place until your death. Unlike the inter vivos trust, there is no need to *fund* a will. The disadvantage of the will is that it must be probated. However, in many cases, the will is the best alternative because of its simplicity and the fact that the court supervises the disposition of assets through the probate process.

Inter Vivos Trusts

The primary purpose of the inter vivos trust is to avoid a court-supervised probate. The inter vivos trust can act as a will substitute by holding title to your assets during your lifetime. Accordingly, upon your death, because the inter vivos trust holds title to your property (instead of you), a probate court need not become involved to issue court orders changing the title to your assets from your name to the names of your estate beneficiaries. During your lifetime, your inter vivos trust can be *amendable*, *revocable*, and entirely for your benefit. Upon your death, your inter vivos trust may terminate, or it may continue in trust for the benefit of your beneficiaries.

Since the assets held by the inter vivos trust are managed by the trustee (usually yourself), if you become incapacitated during your lifetime, the assets in your inter vivos trust can be managed for your benefit by the successor trustee you have selected. This avoids the need of setting a court-supervised *conservatorship* or *guardianship* proceeding in the case of your incapacity.

Although inter vivos trusts have been available and used for generations, they have only become commonplace in the past twenty-five years for several reasons.

- Before the late 1980s, preparation of the inter vivos trust, by typewriter, was prohibitively expensive. An inter vivos trust is a lengthy document, and most people were not inclined to pay for the labor-intensive costs associated with it.
- Attorneys began to advertise about twenty-five years ago. The inter vivos trust, as a product, lends itself well to legal advertising.
- In the early 1980s, the IRS stopped the requirement that inter vivos trusts, during the lifetime of the settlors, use a tax identification number and file a separate income tax return (Form 1041).
- In 1981, Congress passed extensive legislation in the federal estate tax law that made the use of an inter vivos trust more attractive.

Advantages

Some of the advantages of an inter vivos trust include the following.

♦ Inter vivos trusts avoid probate.

♦ An inter vivos trust is less expensive to administer at death than an estate passing through probate.

> **NOTE:** *The trustee often still needs a lawyer to assist and advise in the distribution of the inter vivos trust assets. Generally speaking, there should be a savings in administration costs at death if the inter vivos trust estate is over $300,000, the assets are relatively uncomplicated, the trustee is relatively sophisticated, and the beneficiaries are reasonable.*

♦ An inter vivos trust is a private document, whereas probate records are open to the public. In most states, however, the inter vivos trust terms must be disclosed to the beneficiaries and heirs of the settlor. In other states, the trustee need not disclose the terms of the inter vivos trust unless ordered to do so by the court.

♦ These trusts are convenient for some planning. For example, if you are single and have an estate worth more than $1,500,000 or are a married couple and have an estate worth more than $3,000,000, and you want to utilize the concepts of a *decedent's trust* at your death, then the inter vivos trust is a convenient method to implement your plan.

♦ An inter vivos trust avoids probate in multiple states. While all of your personal property is probated in the state of your residence (regardless of where it is located), real property must be probated in the state in which it is located. An inter vivos trust avoids the need for probate in each state where the settlor owned real property.

Disadvantages

The following are some of the disadvantages of an inter vivos trust.

♦ An inter vivos trust adds a layer of complexity. After you execute your will, you can simply place it in a safe place and forget about it. With an inter vivos trust, the execution is only the first step. After you execute your inter vivos trust, you have to *fund* the inter vivos trust with your assets. Assets not funded in your inter vivos trust may not avoid probate. Furthermore, every time you acquire a new asset, you must be careful to take title in the name of your inter vivos trust. The more your assets change (i.e., the more you buy and sell assets), the more complicated this becomes.

◆ Funding involves executing new deeds to all of your real property and arranging for the change of the title to personal property from your name to the name as trustee of your inter vivos trust.

Example: *Instead of owning your house as "Bob Jones, a single man" the new deed might read "Bob Jones, Trustee of the Bob Jones Trust, dated 4/30/07."*

◆ These trusts are not court-supervised, and thus, a trustee's dishonesty or mistakes are less likely to be discovered.

◆ They are not filed with the court, and may, therefore, be misplaced and unavailable in the future.

◆ It may be more expensive than probate if the assets are complicated or the trustees and beneficiaries do not get along.

In sum, if you have five children, two of whom are minors, who all hate each other, and your estate contains a myriad of assets with a total value under $300,000, forget the inter vivos trust. On the other hand, if you have $1,000,000, all of which is in your personal residence, and have two adult children who get along well, use the inter vivos trust.

Funding Your Inter Vivos Trust

Funding your inter vivos trust is essential. *Funding* means to transfer the title of your assets to your name or names as trustees of your inter vivos trust. For example: "Bob Jones and Mary Jones, Trustees of the Bob Jones and Mary Jones Trust, dated April 2, 2007." Assets *not* funded in the inter vivos trust do *not* avoid probate.

Not all assets need to be transferred. You do not transfer:

- ◆ pension and retirement plans;
- ◆ stock options;
- ◆ life insurance;
- ◆ annuities; or,
- ◆ transfer on death accounts if you are comfortable with their disposal at death.

As to pension and retirement plans, life insurance, annuities, and TOD accounts, you merely need to designate your inter vivos trust as a beneficiary.

NOTE: *If you are married, you generally, for income tax deferral purposes, want to name your spouse as the primary beneficiary on all retirement accounts or pensions. However, your inter vivos trust can be the alternate beneficiary of those assets.*

When naming your inter vivos trust as such a beneficiary, the designation should read, as an example: "The Trustee of the Bob Jones Trust, dated April 2, 2007, to hold, administer, and distribute as to the terms of said trust."

Real Estate

Transferring real estate is very tricky. Each state has its own particular rules. You need to hire someone who is a professional to prepare the deeds to transfer your real estate to your inter vivos trust. If you decide to do it yourself, contact your local county recorder to find out what deed forms are used in your county and if any additional forms need to be filed with the deed. For example, in California, you are required to file a Preliminary Change of Ownership Report with any deed to be recorded.

You must list the *grantors* on the deed to transfer your real property to your inter vivos trust exactly as they are listed on the current deed as *grantees*. For example, the deed to your house lists you as "Bob Jones, a single man." On the new deed, do not list the grantor as "Robert Jones, a married man," but rather as "Bob Jones, a married man who took title as a single man." Also, be sure to take the current title vesting and legal description from the actual current deed, not from a mortgage, deed of trust, or property tax bill, as they can differ from the current deed.

Some lenders in some states consider your transfer of real estate to your inter vivos trust to be a *transfer* that accelerates the *due on sale* provision of your mortgage. To determine your options and avoid problems, check with your lender or use an experienced attorney in your area to handle this chore.

Declaring property to be part of trust in the trust document. Although not recommended, sometimes declaring the property to be an asset of the trust in the inter vivos trust document itself can act to transfer the title of the property to the trust. In California, such a declaration in an inter vivos trust, wherein the settlor is also the trustee, can transfer the asset to the inter vivos trust. (*Estate of Heggstad*, 20 Cal. Rptr. 2d 433 (1993).)

Personal Property

With personal property that has a written title, you need to change title to the name of your inter vivos trust.

With stocks and bonds, you need to contact the transfer agent for the security and follow their instructions for re-titling the securities (it is much easier to first place the securities into a brokerage account first, and then simply change the entire account).

For bank and brokerage accounts, you simply give the brokerage a written instruction to transfer the account to your inter vivos trust, and provide them with either a copy of your inter vivos trust (not a good idea) or a notarized *trust certification* (a summary of your inter vivos trust minus a description of who gets what when you die). Many brokerage houses and banks now require that you use their trust certification form. Included with this book are two forms of a Trust Certification. (see forms 50 and 51 on the CD-ROM.)

For *limited partnership interests,* you need to contact the general partner and request what information he or she will need to transfer your interest to your inter vivos trust. Unless you have very expensive cars or boats, do not bother with transferring them to your inter vivos trust.

Do not place your checking account in your inter vivos trust unless you carry a very large balance in the account. If you do transfer your checking account to your inter vivos trust, do not have the name of your inter vivos trust imprinted on the face of your checks, because identity fraud is easier with a trust than with a person.

Promissory Notes

Execute an ASSIGNMENT of a promissory note from your name to the name of your inter vivos trust. (see form 55 on the CD-ROM.)

Tangible Personal Property

Some lawyers have their clients sign *assignments*, wherein all of their personal, tangible property is assigned to their inter vivos trust. However, such an assignment is probably not effective to tangible, personal property acquired after the date of the assignment. It might be better to simply dispose of that type of property via your *pourover will*.

Using a Will to Create a Trust at Your Death

The following material describes situations in which a will is used to *create* a trust, and provides some useful information regarding these situations.

Testamentary Trust

A *testamentary trust* is a trust created by a will. By definition, it has no effect until the death of the testator of the will. Testamentary trusts are used for several reasons, such as protecting assets from creditors, maximizing estate tax savings, and controlling how your estate is distributed.

Couples with Young Children

Often, couples with young children select an estate plan in which each spouse leaves all of his or her estate to the other spouse, but if there is no surviving spouse, then everything goes into a testamentary trust for the benefit of their minor children. In that event, the spouses name the surviving spouse as the first or primary beneficiary of TOD or POD assets—or contractual assets such as annuities, retirement plans, or life insurance—and then name "the Trustee of the Trust created under my Will dated April 2, 2006, to be held, administered, and distributed per the terms of said Trust" as the second or alternate beneficiary. By naming the testamentary trust created for their children in their wills as the alternate beneficiary, there will be no probate of those life insurance or pension proceeds on the death of the surviving spouse, even though the proceeds pass to the trustee of the testamentary trust.

Tax Planning

As mentioned in Chapter 1, the federal estate tax law exempts the first $2,000,000 of your estate from the federal estate tax when you die. Your estate includes all assets in which you have an ownership interest, including such things as life insurance, pensions, joint tenancy properties, and all gifts you made since 1976 that exceeded the federal annual gift tax exemption amount ($11,000 per year, per gift recipient).

Decedent's Trust

If you own, at your death in 2007, assets worth $3,000,000 for federal estate tax purposes, and you want to leave everything to your children, then the first $2,000,000 will pass federal-estate-tax-free, and the remaining $1,000,000 will incur a federal estate tax of $450,000. However, if you are married, you have options to avoid paying this tax. For purposes of illustration, assume that your spouse has no assets.

Option 1. Leave everything to your spouse. Anything left to a surviving spouse is federal-estate-tax-free. The problem is that upon your spouse's subsequent death, he or she now owns the $3,000,000 in assets, and your children pay $450,000 in federal estate taxes.

Option 2. Leave $1,000,000 of your estate to your spouse and $2,000,000 directly to your children. The $2,000,000 you leave your children passes federal-estate-tax-free, and the $1,000,000 your spouse receives is also federal-estate-tax- free. At your spouse's subsequent death, your children can then receive their $1,000,000 estate free from federal estate taxes.

Option 3. You may not wish to leave the $2,000,000 to your children before the death of your surviving spouse, as you might wish to financially provide for your surviving spouse first. In this case, leave $2,000,000 to a decedent's trust (there is no magic to the name of the decedent's trust—sometimes it is called the *tax credit trust* or the *credit shelter trust* or the *bypass trust*). Although you can have any terms you want as to the distribution to beneficiaries from the decedent's trust, the inter vivos trust forms in this book provide for the decedent's trust to pay all of its income to your surviving spouse, as well as pay principal from the decedent's trust necessary for the support of your surviving spouse in his or her accustomed manner of living. Because your surviving spouse is not, for federal estate tax purposes, the owner of the decedent's trust, the decedent's trust will not be part of his or her estate when he or she later dies, and can pass, federal-estate-tax-free, to your children.

In this option, you leave the other $1,000,000 of your estate to your surviving spouse. At his or her subsequent death, that $1,000,000 can also pass to your children federal-estate-tax-free. By using this option, your surviving spouse has the use of *all* of your estate when you die, and your children save $450,000 in federal estate taxes. What you essentially did was not waste the federal estate tax exemption available at the death of the predeceasing spouse. This third option permitted each spouse to fully utilize his or her federal estate tax exemption.

Marital Trust

In each of the previous three options, the predeceasing spouse left at least $1,000,000 to the surviving spouse *outright* (without any strings attached). Sometimes it is not prudent to leave assets to a surviving spouse outright. An example would be if the surviving spouse is not the parent of your children, and you are concerned that he or she will bequeath whatever you leave that spouse to his or her relatives, and will exclude your children or other relatives. It may be that your surviving spouse is a *spendthrift* (loose with money), has significant money judgments, or has the potential of significant creditors who could claim the money. If your estate is in excess of the federal tax law exemption amount, you can leave a portion or all of that excess into a marital trust.

A marital trust, sometimes called a *QTIP trust*, must:
- ◆ be for the benefit of a surviving spouse;
- ◆ pay all of its income to the surviving spouse; and,
- ◆ give the surviving spouse the right to require the trustee to convert any non-income-producing assets in the marital trust to income-producing assets.

The federal estate tax on the marital trust assets is deferred until the death of your surviving spouse. The marital trust assets are added to the estate of your surviving spouse, and if he or she does not have other assets that fully use up his or her federal estate tax exemption, the marital trust assets use the remainder of the federal estate tax exemption.

Example: *Carlos leaves any estate of $2,800,000, with $2,000,000, in a decedent's trust and $800,000 in a marital trust. At his wife Maria's death in 2007 (federal estate tax exemption in 2007 is $2,000,000), the marital trust is worth $800,000, and Maria leaves $1,200,000 of her own assets at death. As Maria's estate of $1,200,000 leaves $800,000 of her federal estate tax exemption remaining, the marital trust assets of $800,000 are then passed, federal-estate-tax-free, to the persons directed by the predeceasing Carlos.*

Non-Tax Advantages of Decedent's Trusts and Marital Trusts

There are non-tax advantages that sometimes are significant enough to employ the use of a decedent's trust or marital trust even if the estate is under the federal estate tax exemption. First, as previously discussed, use of a decedent's trust or a marital trust, like any trust you create for the lifetime benefit of another, permits you to direct the eventual distribution of assets you left for the benefit of your spouse, after his or her death. This prevents the surviving spouse from lavishing the assets upon his or her new boyfriend, girlfriend, or spouse.

Second, the assets in trust are protected from the creditors of your spouse if you utilize a spendthrift clause in the trust, as is provided in all the forms in this book that create trusts. Third, for larger estates, there is usually a probate cost savings by using an inter vivos trust.

Pension Plans and the Inter Vivos Trust

Pension plans (including IRAs and 401(k)s) are contractual arrangements like life insurance, and thus they pass on death to the contractual beneficiary. Furthermore, ownership to pension plans cannot be transferred to the inter vivos trust, as it would be considered an income taxable distribution. However, naming the inter vivos trust as the beneficiary of the pension plan at the death of the plan participant is often appropriate and can be done with a change of beneficiary form.

Sometimes the value of a person's pension plans make up a substantial portion of a husband's and wife's estate value. If that husband and wife are considering an exemption trust concept to maximize estate tax savings for their children or for non-tax-management reasons, it may be necessary to have the pension plan values included in their estates for purposes of fully funding the decedent's trust. If that is the case, it may be necessary for that husband and wife to execute an agreement that includes the values of the pension plans in funding the decedent's trust.

Example: *Roland and Ashanti, husband and wife, have an estate of $4,000,000, of which $2,000,000 is in Ashanti's IRA. Roland owns $1,000,000 worth of assets and Ashanti owns $1,000,000 worth of non-IRA assets. Roland and Ashanti create an inter vivos trust to hold the $2,000,000 worth of non-IRA assets, and direct in the inter vivos trust that on the death of either spouse, his or her property will go to a decedent's trust, to maximize federal estate tax savings to their children. The maximum permitted in a decedent's trust is $2,000,000. Roland is the named beneficiary of Ashanti's IRA to permit an income tax free spousal rollover if Ashanti dies first. Then Ashanti dies first.*

Ashanti's $1,000,000 worth of inter vivos trust property goes into a decedent's trust. Ashanti's $2,000,000 IRA goes to Roland. Although Ashanti owned $3,000,000 worth of assets, only $1,000,000 funded the decedent's trust instead of the maximum of $2,000,000 worth of assets, as the inter vivos trust only controlled the assets within the inter vivos trust. In this scenario, Roland and Ashanti could have executed an agreement that directed that non-trust assets, such as the IRA, were to be considered in funding the decedent's trust amount at the death of the predeceasing spouse.

If pension plans make up a substantial portion of your estate, and you are considering an inter vivos trust, then you should speak to an estate planning attorney.

Inter Vivos Trusts and the Pourover Will

If you decide to use an inter vivos trust, you still need to also execute a *pourover will* to dispose of your tangible, personal property, as well as any assets that you have not effectively transferred to your inter vivos trust by time of death.

Example: *You believe you have effectively transferred title or ownership of everything you own to your inter vivos trust. You buy a winning lottery ticket and suffer a fatal heart attack upon learning of your newfound riches. The lottery proceeds were not transferred to your inter vivos trust before your death. There will likely be a probate of those lottery proceeds. Your pourover will (forms 21–24) provides that the lottery proceeds would be distributed, after probate, to your inter vivos trust.*

Health Care Powers of Attorney and Directives

In addition to wills and trusts, you may find that you need some additional documents to complete your estate planning. Those documents could include powers of attorney and living wills.

A *durable power of attorney for health care* (DPAHC) or *advance health care directive* (AHCD) permits and directs your agent to make health care decisions concerning you if you are unable or unwilling to do so. As you always have the right to direct your medical treatment if you have capacity (and the law presumes that you have capacity), the power of attorney for health care and advance health care directive are both effective only upon your incapacity. Unlike a power of attorney for financial matters, the DPAHC and AHCD may, depending on the state, extend beyond your death for purposes of authorizing the disposition of remains, autopsy, organ donations, and so on.

Many states have statutory DPAHCs or AHCDs, in which the form to use is expressly stated in the a state law. In many states, medical associations or other state-recognized organizations have fill-in-the-blank DPAHCs or AHCDs. Many of these forms permit the attachment of extra sheets to express wishes or directives if the space otherwise provided for such information is insufficient. It is typically suggested that the statutory or recognized fill-in-the-blank DPAHCs or AHCDs be used, as a health care provider is more readily going to accept them without an independent legal review.

Selection of an Agent

Many states limit who may act as a health care agent. Health care providers, their employees, and operators of community and residential care facilities and their employees are barred from acting as health care agents in some states (a relative of the principal can generally be named as an agent, even if the relative fits in one of these prohibited categories). Married couples usually nominate each other or a child as their agent. Common sense dictates that you obtain the consent of your proposed agent before you nominate him or her. Although an AHCD is a directive, it is also advisable that you discuss your desires regarding your medical care with your agent beforehand. ***Your agent should have a copy of your DPAHC or AHCD.***

Financial Power of Attorney

A *power of attorney* is simply a document giving someone permission to legally act as an *agent* for another person (the person granting the power of attorney to his or her agent is called the *principal*). A *financial power of attorney* is a power of attorney giving someone authority to legally act as your agent on financial matters (instead of health care issues). The financial power of attorney can be *general* (meaning that the agent can act on all financial matters) or it can be *special* or *limited* (meaning that the agent's powers are limited as stated in the document). For example, a special financial power of attorney may permit transactions only on one bank account.

Unless the financial power of attorney expressly states that it is *durable*, the financial power of attorney in most states becomes invalid if the principal becomes mentally incapacitated. Accordingly, most financial powers of attorney expressly state they are durable so they can remain in effect even if the principal becomes mentally incapacitated. In fact, sometimes the principal does not want the agent to have legal authority unless the principal becomes mentally incapacitated. In that situation, the principal might sign a *springing* durable financial power of attorney, which is only good during the principal's mental incapacity (it springs into effect upon the principal's mental incapacity).

Most states provide that the powers of an agent under a general financial power of attorney have some limitations. For example, most states provide that the agent can do nothing that benefits the agent without express authority granted to the agent in the financial power of attorney. Other prohibited powers in various states might include the power to create a trust, execute a will, or make gifts of the principal's property. Many husbands and wives give each other at least a springing durable financial power of attorney, to permit one another to transact financial matters if the other spouse becomes mentally incapacitated.

Financial powers of attorney are readily available in most office supply stores and on the Internet. Further, most states have a permitted financial power of attorney expressly written in their statutes. For example, California Probate Code Section 4401 has a financial power of attorney form directly in the statute.

Since most financial institutions within your state are going to be familiar with your state's statutory form of a financial power of attorney, and the validity of such a financial power of attorney is guaranteed if executed correctly, it makes sense to use the statutory form if one is available in your state and if the form complies with your desires.

To avoid problems with third parties regarding their recognition of the validity of a financial power of attorney, it is wise to consult with known third parties before the execution of the financial power of attorney. For example, if you intend for the agent to have power over your residence and brokerage account, then consult with a title company and brokerage dealer beforehand to see what they will require in the financial power of attorney. A title company may require that the financial power of attorney specifically identify the property, give the agent specific powers, and be recorded within a certain time (i.e., thirty days after execution). A brokerage dealer may have similar or dissimilar requirements. In addition, some third parties may insist that you utilize their financial durable power of attorney form.

A financial power of attorney is generally valid until revoked or until the principal dies. Accordingly, a financial power of attorney is not effective in disposing of one's estate after death. A financial power of attorney can also, on its face, provide for a specific expiration date. In some states, a financial power of attorney will expire, by law, after a certain period of time.

Living Wills

A *living will* is neither a will nor a power of attorney. Instead, a living will expresses your desire not to have your life prolonged by artificial means. The living will does not appoint an agent to carry out your expressed intent. In most states, the living will became a legal document form before the health care power of attorney became legal. Generally speaking, the living will is superceded when the principal executes a health care power of attorney. Some states, including California, have abolished the living will, as it has been replaced by the advance health care directive.

Final Caution

When preparing your will or inter vivos trust, consider the total inheritance of each beneficiary based both upon what that beneficiary receives under your will or inter vivos trust, and what that beneficiary receives outside of the will or inter vivos trust.

Example: *Assume your total estate consists of $400,000 of life insurance, a $500,000 house in your name, and a $100,000 bank account in the name of your inter vivos trust. You want Mary Jones to receive 100% of your estate. However, while Mary Jones is the sole beneficiary under your will, Bob Smith is the sole beneficiary in your life insurance contract, and Billy Jones is the sole beneficiary in your inter vivos trust. At your death, Mary will only receive the house (which accounts for 50% of your estate), Bob will get the life insurance proceeds (40% of the estate), and Billy will get the bank account from the inter vivos trust (10% of the estate). In this case, Mary Jones is actually entitled to only 50% of your estate.*

Chapter 4:

Beneficiaries

This chapter discusses who or what *can* inherit from your will or inter vivos trust, and who or what *cannot* inherit from them. For example, you cannot leave money to your dog, but you could leave money to a friend for the purpose of taking care of your dog. This chapter also discusses the problems in leaving property to minors, persons who are considered disqualified to inherit, and your rights to disinherit.

Who and What Can Inherit?

Three types of entities can inherit from your estate. They are:

- ◆ persons;
- ◆ government; and,
- ◆ nonprofit organizations.

Persons

You can leave your property to any person regardless of age, location, or status.

Example 1: *You can leave your property to a cousin in North Korea. However, North Korea may or may not allow the beneficiary to receive the bequest or may take the bequest from the beneficiary.*

Example 2: *You can leave property to a friend in state prison.*

There are some limitations on this category. In some states, notably California, there are certain persons who are considered to be disqualified to inherit your property unless you take certain prescribed steps to qualify the bequest to them. There are also special considerations to make if the person is a minor.

You do *not* have to leave your one-half interest in *community property* or any of your *separate property* to your spouse or your children. On the other hand, you *cannot* leave your spouse's one-half interest in community property to someone else, as your spouse owns that property. However, nearly every state permits a surviving spouse, regardless of the terms of a decedent's will or inter vivos trust, to take a *forced share* of his or her predeceasing spouse's estate. Accordingly, although you do not have to *leave* a surviving spouse any portion of your estate, the state of your residence may permit your surviving spouse to *take* a portion of your estate. Appendix A summarizes the forced share rights of surviving spouses in the different states.

Government
You can leave your property to any governmental entity in the United States.

Example: *A bequest to the City of Atlanta is legal.*

Nonprofit Organizations
You can leave your property to a nonprofit organization, such as a charity. (See page 59 for information regarding charitable trusts.)

Example: *A bequest to the American Red Cross is legal.*

Who and What Cannot Inherit?
You cannot take it with you, but you cannot leave your property to certain types of organizations or to animals.

Partnerships

You cannot leave your property to a partnership. However, you can leave your property to the *individuals* of a partnership.

Corporations

You cannot leave your property to a for-profit corporation.

Animals

You cannot leave your property to an animal. However, you can leave your property to a person or nonprofit organization in trust to care for an animal.

Special Limitations on Bequests to Minors

If you leave your property to a minor, the court appoints a *guardian* of the minor's estate to manage the *bequest* (and any other asset of the minor) until the minor attains the age of majority (usually 18 years of age, but 21 in some states). At that time, the property is delivered outright to the former minor. Guardianships are safe in that the court-appointed guardian must post a *surety bond* to insure the minor's estate against any dishonesty of the guardian and periodically file an account of the minor's assets with the court.

On the other hand, it costs money to create the guardianship through the court, to obtain a surety bond, and to file the required accountings to the court. However, the biggest problem of guardianships is that they end when the minor attains age of majority. Most 18-year-olds are too young to manage their assets. Fortunately, there are several alternatives to court-supervised guardianships of a minor's estate.

Uniform Transfer to Minors Act

Under the *Uniform Transfer to Minors Act*, sometimes called the *Uniform Gift to Minors Act*, you can bequeath property to an adult person as *custodian* to hold for the benefit of the minor. This is an *informal trust arrangement*. The custodian, who is not under automatic court supervision, is required by law to hold and manage the property for the minor's benefit only. The custodian delivers the property to the minor at an age directed by you—up to age 25.

Example: *"I bequeath $10,000 to Bob Smith, as custodian under the Uniform Transfer to Minors Act, for the benefit of Terry Smith until Terry Smith attains 25 years of age."*

Forms for bequests to a custodian for a minor's benefit are provided on the CD-ROM. Leaving property to a custodian avoids the court costs and court supervision involved in guardianships. Also, the custodians can hold the property for the minor past his or her 18th birthday, if you direct. However, if you fail to specify an age for distribution, the custodian must distribute the property to the former minor when he or she turns 18 or 21 years old, depending on your state. (Check your state's law.)

The disadvantage of custodianships is the lack of mandatory court-filed accountings and bonds. Accordingly, you must be very careful in the selection of the custodian. You should consider requiring that the custodian post a surety bond as a condition of his or her appointment.

I.R.C. 529 College Plans

Congress has enacted legislation that permits states to create and administer college education investment plans. Most investment plans are essentially mutual stock or bond funds. Most states offer different investment options within their plans. Some of the benefits of these plans are:

- ◆ the assets in the plans earn income *tax deferred* (federal and state) until the monies are withdrawn and
- ◆ the income earned is not taxed federally upon withdrawal if the withdrawn funds are used for a *qualified higher educational expense* in college. A qualified higher educational expense includes books, tuition, school room and board, and even many off-campus living expenses.

In an *I.R.C. 529 College Plan*, the *plan contributor* names someone to *control* the plan (i.e., to determine when and what expenses to pay). That person is called the *plan participant.* The beneficiary of the plan is called the *plan beneficiary.* Forms on the CD-ROM permit a custodian or a trustee for a beneficiary to distribute property they manage into a 529 College Plan. Neither the plan contributor, the plan participant, nor the plan beneficiary needs to be a resident of the state where the college plan is opened.

NOTE: *The I.R.C. 529 College Plans can be created by contributions during your lifetime as well.*

Trusts

At your death, you can leave property to a trustee to hold in trust for the benefit of the minor until the minor reaches a more mature age for distribution. In many ways, a *trust* is like custodianship. A trust avoids automatic court involvement and supervision like custodianship. However, unlike a custodianship, a trust can be created for a beneficiary who is not a minor, can delay final distribution beyond age 25, and permits you to place greater conditions and restrictions on the use of the property. For example, you can direct the trustee to pay educational expenses of the beneficiary, or permit the trustee to withhold a distribution if the beneficiary fails a reasonable drug or alcohol abuse test. (See the forms on the CD-ROM for trusts for minors.)

Disqualified Beneficiaries

In what appears to be the wave of the future, California, by statute, disqualifies bequests to certain individuals based upon their involvement in the making of the will, their relationship to the person making the will, or their occupation. California Probate Code Section 21350 disqualifies bequests to:

- ◆ the person who *drafted* the will or inter vivos trust (and the employees, law partners, cohabitants, and certain relatives of said person);
- ◆ any person who has a *fiduciary* relationship with the testator or settlor, who transcribes the will or inter vivos trust, or causes the will or inter vivos trust to be transcribed (and employees, cohabitants, and certain relatives of said persons); and,
- ◆ any *care custodian* of a *dependent adult.*

The disqualified bequest becomes *qualified* if:

- the bequest is $3,000 or less;
- the disqualified person is related by blood to the testator or settlor within five degrees (your parents and children are related to you within one degree, your siblings are related to you within two degrees, a niece or nephew is related to you within three degrees, etc.);
- the disqualified person cohabitates with the testator or settlor (as husband, wife, or gay partner);
- the testator or settlor receives a written *certificate of independent review* of the document from a lawyer after the lawyer reviews the otherwise disqualified transfer with the testator or settlor; or,
- the disqualified person can prove in court by clear and convincing evidence that the bequest was not the product of undue influence, fraud, or duress.

Generally, the disqualified person is involved in the preparation of the will or inter vivos trust in question or is related to the person involved in the preparation of the will. However, the *care custodian* of a *dependent adult* category is a trap for the unwary. The term *care custodian* essentially means anyone who has ever helped an adult. The term *dependent adult* means any person whose mental or physical capacities have diminished at all during his or her lifetime. The care custodian does not have to be involved in the preparation of the will or inter vivos trust in which he or she is left a bequest, and the care custodian does not have to ever give assistance to the testator. In sum, every adult person is a care custodian of a dependent adult. Accordingly, by statute in California, every beneficiary of a will or inter vivos trust is arguably a disqualified person as a care custodian of a dependent adult, unless one of the qualifying exceptions mentioned earlier is met.

Example: *"I leave $5,000.00 to my gardener, Bob Smith." This bequest violates the statute and is disqualified unless the gardener cohabitates with you (as husband, wife, or gay partner) or is related to you within five degrees, or unless you receive a written certificate of independent review as to said bequest from a lawyer.*

Furthermore, the statute is not limited to bequests under a will or inter vivos trust. It also applies to lifetime gift transfers and transfers by trusts, joint tenancies, life insurance, and so on.

– Warning –

An attorney's written certificate of independent review is essential if you want to leave a bequest to a potentially disqualified person.

Although California is the only state to currently have a *disqualified persons* statute, you should be aware of such laws, as they can, if enacted, apply retroactively. Accordingly, if bequests you are considering fall within the California disqualified persons statute, you should consider safeguards, such as the *qualifying* procedures discussed earlier.

Family Changes after Execution of the Will

In many states, a spouse or child *acquired* after the date of the execution of a will is considered to be *forgotten* by the testator, and therefore, entitled to his or her intestate succession share of the testator's estate.

Example: *Bob, a single man with one child, executes a will leaving everything to his one child. Bob then marries Sue. Bob dies on his honeymoon with Sue, without amending or executing a new will. In many states, Sue is now entitled to the share of Bob's estate that she would have received if Bob had no will, regardless of the fact that Bob's will leaves everything to his one child.*

Who Can You Disinherit?

You do not have to leave your estate to someone you do not want to, even if that person is your spouse or your child. You have the right to *disinherit* anyone. However, nearly every state has a *forced share* statute that provides for a share of your estate to pass to a surviving spouse. (see Appendix A.)

Disinheritance Clause

Paragraph THIRD of the will forms and Paragraph 6.17 of the inter vivos trust forms in this book use a comprehensive disinheritance clause that disinherits all persons other than those specifically named as beneficiaries in the will. Accordingly, if someone shows up after your death claiming to be your long-lost brother, he is still subject to the disinheritance clause and would receive no part of your estate.

Who Can Contest Your Will or Your Inter Vivos Trust?

Although you have the right to disinherit anyone, certain persons can contest your will or inter vivos trust by claiming:

- ◆ that the will or inter vivos trust was improperly executed;
- ◆ that you lacked mental competency to execute a will or inter vivos trust;
- ◆ that the will or inter vivos trust was the result of fraud; or,
- ◆ that the will or inter vivos trust was the result of undue influence.

Only certain persons have the right to contest your will or inter vivos trust. The persons are:

- ◆ those persons who would take your estate if there were no will or inter vivos trust (your heirs), and
- ◆ those persons who received a bequest from you under a prior will or inter vivos trust.

Example: *You are single with one adult child. Your child has two children. Your first and only will leaves everything to your brother. Your child, the person who would take your property if there were no will, has the legal right to contest your will. Your grandchildren do not have the right to contest your will, as they would not inherit your property if your will was declared to be invalid because their parent (your child) survived you.*

Anti-Contest Clause

In the second part to paragraph THIRD of the wills or Paragraph 6.17 of the inter vivos trusts included in this book is an *anti-contest clause* that disinherits not only anyone who contests the will or inter vivos trust, but also anyone who contests transfers—such as joint tenancies, TOD securities accounts, or life insurance. It even disinherits persons who make claims against your estate for services rendered or agreements to share property.

Therefore, the only persons truly affected by the anti-contest clause are the persons who have something to lose under your will or inter vivos trust if they contest it and lose (i.e., the beneficiaries).

Example: *A beneficiary who receives 10% of your estate under your will or inter vivos trust but who would be entitled to 25% of your estate if you died without a will is affected by the anti-contest clause. A decision then must be made to either not contest the will or inter vivos trust and take the 10% or contest the will or inter vivos trust and possibly lose the 10%.*

The anti-contest clause does not prohibit anyone from contesting the will—it simply states that anybody who does contest your will is disinherited. If a person is not a beneficiary of your estate, he or she has nothing to lose under the anti-contest clause.

Bequest Incentives to Avoid Contests

Will or inter vivos trust contests are messy and expensive legal matters. Yet, as discussed above, the anti-contest clause only helps to prevent will contests by persons who have something to lose. Accordingly, if you want to disinherit an *heir* (a person who would take a portion or all of your estate if there was no will), consider leaving that heir a small bequest as an incentive not to contest the will or inter vivos trust.

Example: *You dislike your son, one of the two heirs to your estate, and want to leave all of your property to your other heir. However, you know that the disinherited son will contest your will simply to exact an emotional and financial toll on the beneficiary of your property. You could decide to leave the son you dislike $10,000 in your will with the anti-contest clause. At your death, the son you dislike now has a dilemma. If he contests the will and loses, he also loses the $10,000 bequest.*

Obviously, the amount of the bequest incentive will differ depending on the value of your estate and the potential anger of the person.

Chapter 5:

Bequests

Each time you dispose of property in your will or inter vivos trust, you are said to be making a *bequest*. The act of making a bequest is to *bequeath*. Historically, a bequest was a gift in a will of personal property and a *devise* was a gift in a will or inter vivos trust of real estate. Certain states may call all gifts in a will or inter vivos trust either devises or bequests. However, because of the common usage of the word bequest, that term is used exclusively in this book.

This chapter discusses three separate and often intermingled topics about bequests. First, it discusses the difference between a *specific bequest* and a *residual bequest*. As part of that topic, the differences among *tangible personal property*, *intangible personal property*, and *real property* are discussed.

Finally, this chapter will discuss various ways property can be left to beneficiaries. Those ways include:
- ◆ outright (no strings attached);
- ◆ with conditions;
- ◆ in a life estate; or,
- ◆ in trust (including custodianships).

Specific and Residual Bequests

Regardless of other categorizations, bequests are either *specific* or *residual*.

Specific Bequests

In *specific bequests*, the property bequeathed is specifically identified by item (e.g., "my 1974 Ford Pinto"), by type (e.g., "all of my household furnishings"), or by amount (e.g., "$100,000"). Specific bequests can be further described by the type of property.

Tangible personal property. Personal property you can touch, move, or hold—such as cars, clothes, or household items—is called *tangible personal property*. Specifically bequeathing identified items of tangible, personal property, such as "the pink couch in my living room," is discouraged for several reasons.

- First, said items may be sold, discarded, or gifted before your death, which then raises the question whether the beneficiary is to get the new green couch in your living room.
- Second, if the specifically identified property cannot be found after your death, your executor must either explain to the court if he or she knows what happened to the property or make diligent efforts to locate the specifically identified property and then describe those efforts to the court.
- Finally, if you do own the specifically identified property at the time of your death, your executor will have to have it separately appraised and separately inventoried on any federal estate tax returns filed with the IRS. Any probate inventories filed with the probate court may result in an increased value (bad for tax purposes), as well as an additional cost of appraisal. Sometimes the cost of appraisal can exceed the value of the item.

On the other hand, a beneficiary of your highly valued Van Gogh painting may want it to be specifically devised, appraised, and inventoried for income tax basis purposes, insurance purposes, and to later be able to prove how he or she acquired title to the painting.

In paragraph SECOND of the will forms, you have the opportunity to make a specific bequest of tangible personal property. Therefore, you *can* bequeath your Van Gogh painting or pink couch in your living room if you wish.

After the listing of any specific bequests of tangible personal property, paragraph SECOND permits you to bequeath the remaining tangible personal property (or all of it, if you made no specific bequests) to one or more persons or entities, in equal shares.

Occasionally, the division of the tangible personal property among the family members can be the most troublesome part of the distribution of your estate. Although the dollar amount may be small, sentimental attachment or long-term resentments are often involved. In those situations, you may wish to prepare an informal note advising the beneficiaries of how you want certain items of tangible, personal property to be distributed. Keep that note with your will. Although the note may not be legally enforceable, it could guide reasonable beneficiaries.

Intangible personal property. *Intangible personal property* includes cash, securities, partnership interests, promissory notes, and business interests that are merely representative of value. Paragraph SECOND in the will forms permits the bequeathing of intangible personal property.

Bequests of specific, noncash, intangible personal property, such as five hundred shares of IBM stock, are discouraged, as the stock could, before your death, be sold, have a 3 for 1 stock split, or change substantially in value. Remember that a will speaks as of the date of death. On the other hand, cash bequests, assuming the cash will be available at your death, are not a problem.

Example: *"I bequeath $10,000 to Bob Smith" is an acceptable bequest of intangible personal property.*

Real property. Improved and unimproved real estate, including mineral interests and condo stock co-ops, are all *real property*. The bequeathing of specific parcels of real property is also discouraged, as it may be sold or exchanged before your death, or its value or mortgage encumbrances may materially change from time to time.

However, paragraph SECOND of the will forms in this book permits bequeathing specific real property. If such a bequest is made, you must decide whether the real property is to be distributed to the beneficiary subject to all mortgages on the real property or whether your estate is to pay off the mortgages for the beneficiary.

Residual Bequests

Residual bequests dispose of the residue of your estate. The *residue* is what is left in the estate after payment of all costs of the administration of your estate, all of your debts, and all of your specific bequests in your will. In many wills or inter vivos trusts, the residue is the largest portion of the estate, and sometimes, in those cases where there are no specific bequests, the residue is the entire estate. Because the residue includes what is left, it includes both real property and all types of personal property.

If there is more than one residual beneficiary, you need to determine what portion of the residue each beneficiary is to receive. The interest of each beneficiary need not be the same as another.

Example: *"I leave Bob 10% of the residue and Mary 90% of the residue."*

Instead of listing the interest of each beneficiary in terms of a percentage of the residue, using *shares* is recommended. The reason to use shares is because one or more of the residual beneficiaries might die before you. If each share represents a fraction of the residue, then regardless of whether any shares lapse, it is easy to determine what each beneficiary receives. You might find this concept easier to conceptualize if you start with one hundred shares—each share then equals 1%. If a bequest of five shares, for example, lapses due to the death of the beneficiary before you, then there are ninety-five shares, and each share is worth $\frac{1}{95}$—slightly more than 1%.

Example: *"I devise all of the rest of my estate as follows:*

A. Twenty-five shares to Bob Smith;
B. Ten shares to Mary Jones; and,
C. Sixty-five shares to John Doe.

If any of the above persons die before my death, their devise shall lapse."

If all three beneficiaries survive you, Bob will get 25% of the residue, Mary will get 10% of the residue, and John will get 65% of the residue. If Bob and Mary survive the decedent, but John does not, then Bob will get 25/35 of the residue (about 78%) and Mary will get 10/35 (about 22%).

Conditional Outright Bequests

So far, unconditional outright bequests have been discussed. However, outright bequests can have conditions attached. Generally, conditions are *conditions precedent*, that is, conditions that must be met before delivery of the bequest. For example, a condition that a bequest not be paid until the beneficiary graduates from a university is valid.

Conditions cannot be illegal or against public policy. For example, a condition that the beneficiary do an illegal act—such as murder someone—would be illegal and not enforceable. A condition that the beneficiary not marry anyone of Hungarian heritage would also be a violation of anti-discrimination laws, and thus, unenforceable. However, a condition that a beneficiary not marry a specific individual *is* enforceable. This author recommends *against* imposing any conditions to bequests; however, if you wish to do so, you should seek the expertise of a lawyer.

The most common condition to a bequest is that of surviving the testator by a certain period of time. (Where applicable, the will forms in this book have used a thirty-day *survivorship* requirement.)

Life Estates

Sometimes you want the beneficiary to have only the right to use the property for his or her lifetime, and then have the property distributed to a second beneficiary after the death of the first beneficiary. The beneficiary using the property for his or her lifetime is called the *life tenant*. The beneficiary who takes the property after the death of the life tenant is called the *remainderman.*

Although any type of property can be subject to a life estate, the most common situation involves the use of real property.

Example: *You bequeath your daughter a life estate in your residence. Your daughter has the right to use your residence after your death, for the remainder of her lifetime. Your daughter could live in the residence, rent the residence to others (however, she could not rent the residence for a period of time beyond her lifetime), or even sell her life estate (the buyer of a life estate buys only the right to use the property during the lifetime of the selling life tenant).*

During her life estate, your daughter, as the life tenant, would pay all interest (but not principal) on any encumbrance on the property, association dues, normal repairs, insurance, and property taxes.

After the death of the life tenant, the remainderman becomes the absolute owner of the property. Sometimes, in a second marriage situation, the predeceasing spouse leaves the surviving spouse a life estate in the predeceasing spouse's residence, with the remaindermen being the children of the predeceasing spouse's prior marriage.

Testamentary Trusts

Many different *testamentary trusts* (trusts created at your death by will or inter vivos trust) exist, and are used to hold your assets at death for the benefit of others. The testamentary trusts utilized in the will and inter vivos forms in this book are used to manage assets for the benefit of one beneficiary until he or she either receives the trust assets upon attaining a designated age or he or she dies and the trust estate is delivered to a second beneficiary—or in the case of a surviving spouse, to save federal estate taxes.

In many ways, the trusts used in the will and inter vivos trust forms contained in this book work like the life estate previously discussed, with some exceptions.

◆ A trust is a more convenient method of handling a group of assets, especially a residual interest in an estate, rather than multiple life estates—one for each property.

◆ A trust places the legal title to property in the hands of a trustee to manage for the beneficiary, rather than relying on the beneficiary to properly manage the property. (In many cases, the beneficiary is too financially unsophisticated to manage the property.)

◆ The trust provides flexibility in distributions during the life of the trust and can provide for distributions to the beneficiary upon the beneficiary attaining a specified age.

The will or inter vivos trust forms on the CD-ROM provide for trusts of residual shares of the estate for a spouse, child, or friend. Some of the will forms provide for the beneficiary to receive discretionary payment of principal for illnesses as well as the *income* of the trust. If you want greater flexibility with the distributions from the trust to the beneficiaries, you need to consult with a lawyer to draft your will or inter vivos trust. Of course, as with any bequest in your will or inter vivos trust, the funding and administration of the trust created by your will or inter vivos trust does not occur until after your death.

Charitable Trusts

There are times when a person does not want to make an outright gift during his or her lifetime or an outright bequest at death to a charity, but still wishes to eventually benefit the charity.

If the issue is a lifetime gift, the charity will often accept a gift in a *charitable remainder trust*. In a charitable remainder trust, the gift is given to the charity or to a trustee, who then pays the donor (person making the gift) an annual amount of cash until the donor dies. In essence, the donor gets a guaranteed cash flow in consideration of his or her gift, and the charity gets the gift less whatever is paid to the donor during the donor's lifetime.

Example: *Bob, who is 90 years old, gives John Doe Memorial Hospital (a qualified charitable institution) $100,000 in a charitable remainder trust that will pay to Bob, during his lifetime, the monthly sum of $600. Using the annuity tables set for the in I.R.C. Treasury Regulations Sections 25.2512-5 and 25.7520-1 through 25.7520-4, and assuming the I.R.C. Section 7520 midterm rate is 6%, then the value of the gift to the charity would be $74,190, which Bob could take as an income tax deduction. In addition, at Bob's death the gift would not be included in his estate, as the charity owns the gift.*

If Bob had instead made such a gift effective at his death, with the $600 per month going to his sister, who was 90 years of age, the result would be the same. Included in his estate for federal estate tax purposes would be $25,810 (the value of his sister's annuity), and the other $74,190 going to the charity would not be subject to tax.

However, as good as a charitable remainder trust sounds, very stringent I.R.C. rules must be followed to obtain any federal tax benefit when creating a charitable remainder trust. As an example, if Bob had bequeathed $100,000 in trust, with the income of the trust to go to his sister, and upon his sister's death, the $100,000 to go to Joe Doe Memorial Hospital, no federal tax benefit would have been allowed. A charitable remainder trust, to have federal tax advantages, cannot simply pay its income to a beneficiary. To be effective, a charitable remainder trust must either be a *unitrust* or an *annuity trust*. A *unitrust* pays a set percentage of the value of the trust assets each year to the noncharitable beneficiary. For example, if 4% of the value of the trust, re-valued each year, was paid to the noncharitable beneficiary, then it would be a unitrust. An *annuity trust* pays a fixed-dollar amount annually to the noncharitable beneficiary. For example, $5,000 per year is paid to the noncharitable beneficiary.

Obviously, the value of the charitable gift or bequest is dependent upon the age of the noncharitable beneficiary (the older the noncharitable beneficiary, the larger the charitable gift or bequest), interest rates at the time of the gift or bequest (the higher the interest rate, the greater the charitable gift or bequest), and the amount of the payment (the smaller the payment for an annuity charitable remainder trust or the smaller the percentage for a unitrust charitable remainder trust, the larger the charitable gift or bequest).

Not all charitable trusts have to be remainder trusts (in which the charity takes after the death of a noncharitable beneficiary). Another type of charitable trust is called a *charitable lead trust*, in which the charity receives the assets before the noncharitable beneficiary.

Example: *Bob owns 80% of the stock in ABC company. His stock is worth $10,000,000. Bob does not want his heirs to have to sell the stock at his death, as he wants them to be able to continue to control the company. Bob creates a charitable lead trust that provides that upon his death, his ABC company shares will go to the charity for fifteen years and then revert back to his heirs. During that fifteen years, the charity receives 7% of the value of the trust. Bob is confident that the trustee will not sell the ABC company stock and will instead enjoy its dividend. Assuming the I.R.C. Section 7520 midterm rate is 6% at Bob's death, the value of the lead bequest to the charity would be $6,800,000, and Bob's heirs get the property back in fifteen years.*

Due to the complexities involved in drafting a valid charitable remainder trust or charitable lead trust, it is highly recommended that you consult with an attorney. Many charitable organizations will either recommend attorneys who have expertise in this specialty or will actually pay the legal fees for the preparation of the charitable remainder trust.

Chapter 6:

Fiduciary Positions

A *fiduciary* is someone who owes a duty of loyalty and fairness to another. It is a position of trust, wherein the fiduciary cannot take a financial or personal advantage. This chapter discusses three types of fiduciaries: the guardian, the executor, and the trustee or custodian.

Guardian

You have the right to nominate a *guardian* to care for your minor children after your death. There are two types of guardians. First, there is the guardian of the *person*. The guardian of the person is responsible for the minor's housing, food, clothing, and so on. Then there is the guardian of the *estate*. The guardian of the minor's estate manages any assets of the minor that are not managed by a custodian or a trustee.

Only people can be appointed by the court to be a guardian of a minor's person. However, trust companies and people can be appointed by the court to be a guardian of a minor's estate. The guardian of the person and the guardian of the estate do not have to be the same person. Although a *guardianship estate* of a minor can be substantial, many times, the assets of the minor are in the hands of the *custodians* or *trustees* (discussed later in this chapter). Guardianships of person and estate both end when the minor attains the age of majority in their state of residence (usually 18 years of age).

You have the right to nominate a guardian for your children only if there is no natural parent of the minor living (unless the natural parent is legally determined to be unfit). Simply because you are the divorced, custodial parent of your child does not mean that you have the sole right to nominate a guardian for your minor children in the event of your demise.

In most states, minors aged 14 years and older have the right to express a preference for the guardian of their person. You, the parent of the minor, have only the right to *nominate* a guardian. Only the court can *appoint* a guardian. Although the court will consider your written nomination of a guardian, the court's appointment of the guardian will be based upon what the court determines to be *in the best interest of the minor*. In short, your nomination of a guardian is not legally binding on the court.

Selection of the Guardian of the Person

Obviously, it is wise to verify with a prospective guardian that he or she is willing to act. In addition, you must be comfortable with the lifestyle choices of the prospective guardian. Sometimes your best friends would make the worst guardians. In selecting a guardian of the person for a minor child, consider the following questions.

- *Does the guardian live near the minor's family members?* It might be wiser to select your cousin, who lives near the minor's family members, than a sister who lives on the other side of the nation.
- *Is there religious compatibility between the guardian and your child?*
- *If the child is older, is the proximity of the guardian's residence to the friends and school of the child important?*
- *What is the age of the prospective guardians?* Your mother may be too old to handle your minor child.
- *What is the family situation of the guardian?* Your friends with the 2-year-old quintuplets might be too busy with their children to act as guardians for your 13-year-old twins.
- *Is the issue of divorce a consideration on your selection?* If you choose Mary Smith, who is married at the time of the nomination, do you still want her to act if, at the time of your death, she is divorced or married to someone new?

◆ *Is there a problem of nominating a husband and wife as co-guardians? Which one might or should continue as guardian if they divorce after your death?* Consider nominating only the husband or the wife as guardian to avoid confusion over your intent in the event that husband and wife later divorce.

Instructions to the Nominated Guardian

As the court acts in the best interest of the child, the nominated guardian should be aware beforehand of the nomination, and should have at least one copy of your NOMINATION OF GUARDIAN for his or her use if necessary. (see form 1 on the CD-ROM.) You need to tell the proposed guardian that, in the event of your death, no one is automatically going to hand him or her your children and the court is not going to appoint him or her without the proposed guardian petitioning the court to do so. In the event of your death, the nominated guardian needs to immediately take physical possession of the minors and petition the court for temporary guardianship of each minors' person, pending the court hearing on the appointment of the permanent guardian.

Persons you might *not* want to act as guardians for your children often become the guardians simply because they acted more quickly than the deceased parent's nominated guardian. Many judges refuse to move a minor child from the custody of the first person to take possession of the child after the death of the child's parent to avoid a further disruption of the minor child's life.

Use of the Nomination of Guardian Forms

The two NOMINATION OF GUARDIAN forms (form 1 and form 2) in this book are designed to be used independent of the will. Using a separate NOMINATION OF GUARDIAN form does not give the proposed guardian a copy of your will.

The first form is your basic guardianship nomination form when you do not expect any conflict over the nomination. The second form should be used when you suspect there may be a conflict over the appointment of the guardian, and the appointment of a particular guardian is of the utmost importance to you. Both forms provide that the same person is nominated to act as guardian of your minor child's person *and* estate.

Executor

An *executor* is the person or *corporate fiduciary* (trust company) that is appointed under your will to manage your estate after you die. The executor will:

◆ offer your will to the court for probate;

◆ marshal your assets;

◆ file an inventory of your assets with the court;

◆ pay all debts, expenses of administration, and taxes; and,

◆ sell any property that must be sold to put the estate in a position to be closed.

The executor will petition the court to make an order to distribute your estate. During the probate of your estate, the executor has the duty to account for the financial transactions of the estate and to keep the court and the beneficiaries informed as to the progress of the estate administration. After the court issues the order for distribution, the executor will distribute your estate pursuant to the terms of the order that incorporates the asset disposition provisions of your will.

The term *executor* means that the person or trust company was appointed under a will. If the person or trust company is not named under a will, then that person or trust company is called an *administrator*. Years ago, those terms referred only to men or trust companies. Women were referred to as an *executrix* or an *administratrix*. In recent years, there has been a tendency to refer to executors, executrixes, administrators, and administratrices simply as *personal representatives.*

A will does not have to nominate an executor to be valid. However, nomination in your will of the executor permits you to select the executor and to determine whether the executor should be bonded or not.

Selecting Your Executor

Carefully select your executor. Too many people feel that the job is merely honorary and that competence is a secondary consideration. Nothing could be further from the truth. A good executor will make the difference between an estate that is handled efficiently and expeditiously versus an estate that will get mired in eventual litigation and losses. A good executor is one who keeps detailed financial records, is not a procrastinator, and can make difficult decisions. Although the executor will most likely hire a lawyer for assistance, the responsibility begins with and ends with the executor.

If you do not have someone you trust and who fits the above description to select as your executor, consider naming a trust company to act as the executor. Many banks have trust companies as part of their operations. The primary objections to trust companies are that they are impersonal and they charge the maximum statutory fee permitted. However, being impersonal can be a good thing, and many family members or friends who act as executor also take the statutory fee, as being an executor is work and the fee is earned.

Trust companies are professionals. They have created systems to keep track of all transactions and the progress of the estate. They do not wait until the end of the month to make income deposits; they keep records of financial transactions; and, they do not steal the estate assets. However, if your estate is under $200,000, most trust companies will decline to act, as the statutory fee is too small. If you select a trust company as your executor, you may wish to discuss the matter with them beforehand, contract a fee agreement with them, and even give them a copy of your will. However, you do not have to contact the trust company before your death.

Surety Bonds

Many lawyers will tell you that if you cannot trust a person enough to waive the requirement of posting a *surety bond* as the executor, then you should not appoint that person as the executor. However, bonds often help keep an executor honest, and no honest executor should object to posting a surety bond.

The surety bond posted by the executor is an amount equal to the value of the personal property of estate (real property does not have to be bonded, as it cannot be sold without consent of the beneficiaries or the court). It is an inexpensive form of insurance to guarantee that the executor will act honestly. The cost of such a bond is relatively modest (i.e., $500 per year for a $200,000 bond), but adds financial protection to the estate and the benefit of the concern of the bonding company.

The bonding company does not want to lose money. Accordingly, the bonding company checks the credit rating of the executor and sometimes requires the executor to give the bonding company joint control over major estate assets to lessen the bonding company's liability exposure. Bonds are especially important when minors are beneficiaries of the estate, as they usually are unable to ascertain if the estate is being mishandled or not.

Waiver of Publication

In the will forms in this book, paragraph FOURTH is the nomination of executor paragraph. In that paragraph, you waive the requirement of publishing a legal notice in a newspaper each time the executor wishes to sell estate property. Publication requirements differ from state to state. However, where required, publication is a formality that costs money and time, but does not protect the estate or assist in obtaining the highest price for the property sold. In most states, the waiving of the publication requirement *does not* give the executor the right to sell property without either the permission of all affected beneficiaries under the will or the permission of the court.

Trustee

As described, the executor manages the estate after your death and during the probate process. On the other hand, the *trustee* of a trust created in a will (a testamentary trust) receives, from the executor of your will, property at the end of the probate of your estate, and then manages that property.

A trustee of an inter vivos trust (one created by you during your lifetime) administers the property in that inter vivos trust for the benefit of the trust's beneficiaries that are named in it. This trustee might be acting during your lifetime (i.e., you could be incapacitated or simply not wish to be bothered with the management of your estate) or after your death.

The trustee has legal title to the property under his or her control, and can buy or sell assets without permission from the court or the beneficiaries (unless, under the terms of the trust, permission from the court or beneficiaries is required). Unlike an executor, the trustee is not automatically under the jurisdiction of the court. Like an executor, the trustee must render accountings to the beneficiaries and must keep the beneficiaries informed. The trustee is entitled to reasonable compensation for his or her services, but may make no other profit at the expense of the trust (i.e., a trustee may not receive a commission on trust property he or she sells).

Unlike the short tenure of an executor (it takes about one year to probate an estate), a trustee might act for a substantial number of years. In addition, unlike an executor, a trustee generally does not rely upon an attorney for the day-to-day management of the trust.

You should take even greater concerns about the appointment of your trustee, as he or she holds the assets for a greater period of time and the court does not supervise trustees. Only consider persons who are financially sophisticated, extremely conscientious, and keep excellent financial records. Being a trustee is a job itself, so be sure the person you nominate has the time.

It is advisable to nominate multiple trustees (usually two), called *co-trustees,* and to require the trustees to post a surety bond. If you do not have someone you trust who fits the above description to select as your trustee, then consider naming a trust company (many banks have trust companies as part of their operations).

Just as a trust company acting as your executor charges a fee, a trust company acting as trustee will charge a fee. The fee is usually about 1% annually of the value of the trust assets. To avoid this fee, some people name family members or friends as trustees. However, family members or friends may decide to take a fee larger than what a trust company would, and they do not have the financial systems or expertise that the trust company has.

If you are considering the appointment of a trust company to handle your trust, interview several trust companies to learn more about their employees (trust officers), their methods of doing business (i.e., financial management viewpoint), and their fee schedule. Sometimes the fee schedule can be negotiated in advance and can protect your estate from unhappy surprises.

Custodian

Custodians are like trustees, except that custodians are limited to handling assets of persons under the age of 25 years (the maximum age can differ from state to state). Custodians hold assets transferred to a minor under the *Uniform Transfer to Minors Act*. Custodians are not automatically under court supervision.

Conclusion of Fiduciary Positions

The appointment of your fiduciaries is not to be taken lightly. The best-planned will or trust may disintegrate in the hands of an incompetent or dishonest fiduciary. Selecting the best guardian, executor, trustee, or custodian is more important than being concerned over hurting the feelings of a friend or family member. Additional care must be exercised when the trustee you are considering might have to act during your lifetime due to your incapability, as you could then personally feel the pain of an unqualified or dishonest trustee.

Chapter 7:

Execution, Safekeeping, and Revocation of Wills and Inter Vivos Trusts

This chapter will explain the formalities required to properly execute your will or inter vivos trust; give suggestions for the safekeeping of your will or inter vivos trust; and, discuss the steps needed to revoke your will or inter vivos trust.

Will Execution

The actual requirements for will execution differ from state to state. However, the following instructions are legal in each state except Louisiana. The requirements for Louisiana are explained throughout the discussion of the execution of wills.

Self-Proving Wills

Nearly all states permit the admission of uncontested wills to probate without testimony of a witness to the will, as long as the will is *self-proving* under the law of that state. A will that is not self-proving is not inadmissible or invalid. Such wills simply need the testimony of a witness (or evidence that a witness cannot be found and then other evidence, such as the testimony of a person familiar with the decedent's handwriting, that the signature of the decedent on the will is in the handwriting of the decedent). However, because self-proving wills are easier to have admitted to probate by the court, you should, whenever possible, take the necessary steps to have your will be self-proving.

In California, a will is self-proving if the witnesses attest, under penalty of perjury, that the will was properly executed. (Each of the will forms and the codicil form in this book comply with California's self-proving statute.)

All states use a SELF-PROVING AFFIDAVIT. The specific form number on the CD-ROM is provided for each state in the following paragraphs (except California, because, as already mentioned, all forms in this book comply with California's self-proving statute).

Alabama, Alaska, Arizona, Arkansas, Colorado, Connecticut, Florida, Hawaii, Idaho, Illinois, Indiana, Maine, Michigan, Minnesota, Mississippi, Nebraska, Nevada, New Jersey, New Mexico, New York, North Carolina, North Dakota, Oregon, Pennsylvania, South Carolina, South Dakota, Tennessee, Utah, Washington, West Virginia, Wisconsin, and Wyoming all use form 25.

Delaware, Georgia, Kansas, Kentucky, Massachusetts, Missouri, Oklahoma, and Virginia use form 26.

Texas uses form 27. New Hampshire uses form 28. Louisiana uses form 29. Iowa uses form 30. Montana uses form 31. Rhode Island uses form 32.

As states tend to change their self-proving affidavits from time to time, contact a notary in your state to obtain the most recent self-proving affidavit for your state.

In the District of Columbia, Maryland, Ohio, and Vermont, self-proving wills are either unnecessary or not recognized.

States Using Form 25

Alabama Code Section 43-8132

Alaska Statutes 13.12.504

Arizona Code Section 14-2504

Arkansas Code 28-25-106

Colorado Code Section 15-11-504

Connecticut General Statute Section 45a-251

Florida Statutes Annotated Section 732.503

Hawaii Revised Statutes Section 560:2-504

Idaho Statutes 15-2-504

Illinois: 755 Illinois Compiled Statutes
Section 5/6-4 (Illinois permits nearly any
of the self-proving affidavits forms
provided in this book)

Indiana Code 29-1-5-3.1 (Indiana does not
expressly authorize this form but this
form satisfied the requirements of the
Indiana Code)

Maine Statutes Section 2-504 (Title 18A)

Michigan Compiled Laws Annotated Section
700.2504

Minnesota Statutes Section 524.2-504

Mississippi Code Section 91-707 (requires
addresses of witnesses to be added)

Nebraska Revised Statutes Section 30-2329

Nevada Revised Statutes 133.150 (Nevada
permits nearly any of the self-proving
affidavit forms in this book, but must be
notarized)

New Jersey Statutes Annotated Sections 3B:
3-4 and 3B: 3.5

New Mexico Statutes 45.2.504

New York Surrogate's Court Procedure,
Section 1406 (New York permits nearly
any of the self proving forms in this
book, but must be notarized)

North Carolina General Statutes Section 31-
11.6(a)

North Dakota Statutes 30.1-08-04

Oregon Revised Statutes Section 113.055
(Oregon permits nearly any of the self
proving forms in this book)

Pennsylvania Statutes Annotated – Title 20
Section 3132.1

South Carolina Statutes Section. 62-2-503

South Dakota Codified Laws Section 29A-2-
504

Tennessee Annotated Code Section 32-2-110
(Tennessee permits nearly any of the self
proving forms in this book, must be
notarized)

Utah Code Section 75-20504

Washington Revised Code Annotated 11.20-
020 (Washington permits nearly any of
the self proving forms in this book, must
be notarized)

West Virginia Code Section 41-5-15 (West
Virginia permits nearly any of the self
proving forms in this book, must be
notarized).

Wisconsin Statutes Chapter 853.04

Wyoming Statutes Annotated Section 2-6-
114

States Using Form 26

Delaware Code Section 1305

Georgia Code Section 53-4-24

Kansas Code Section 59-606

Kentucky Acts 394.225

Massachusetts General Laws Annotated
Chapter 192 Section 2

Missouri Annotated Statutes Section 474.337

Oklahoma Statutes Annotated Title 84
Section 55

Virginia Code Section 64.1-87.1

States Using Form 27
Texas Probate Code Annotated Section 59

States Using Form 28
New Hampshire Revised Statutes Annotated
    Section 551:2-a

States Using Form 29
Louisiana Civil Code Section 1577

States Using Form 30
Iowa Code Section 633.279

States Using Form 31
Montana Code Annotated Section 72-2-524

States Using Form 32
Rhode Island General Laws 33-7-26

To execute your will, do the following.

◈   Step One: Optional—Have a notary present. (The notary cannot be one of your witnesses.) *In Louisiana, this step is mandatory.*

◈   Step Two: The *testator* announces, in the presence of two (in Vermont, there must be three) adult, competent witnesses (who are not beneficiaries or relatives of beneficiaries of the will), that:

  • the testator has read the will;
  • the testator understands the provisions of the will; and,
  • the will disposes of the testator's property in the manner that the testator wants.

Example: *"This is my will. I have read it. I understand it. It disposes of my property in a manner that I want it to be disposed of at my death."*

NOTE: *This announcement should also be made in front of the notary if one is present. Remember—the notary cannot be one of the witnesses.*

◈   Step Three: In the presence of the witnesses, the testator signs the will at the end of the signature paragraph (but before the witnesses' signatures) and dates the will. The signature paragraph is very short. It simply reads: "In Witness hereof I set my hand hereto on this _____ day of _____, 20_____," and then has a place for the signature of the testator.

◈   Step Four: In the presence of the witnesses, the testator initials the bottom of each page of the will. *In Louisiana, the testator must sign each page.*

◈   Step Five: The witnesses each read the *attestation clause* in the will, and then date and sign in the presence of the testator, and then in the presence of each other. The witnesses should print their names under their signed names if their handwriting is difficult to read. They should also include their addresses. *In Louisiana, the will must be notarized as well as have witnesses.*

◈   Step Six: All witnesses initial each page.

Step Seven: The testator and witnesses complete the *self-proving affidavit* (where necessary) under the supervision of the notary.

Duplicate Originals

You may execute more than one original will. Execute the duplicates at the same time, with the same witnesses present.

Execution of Inter Vivos Trust

The settlor has his or her signature at the end of the inter vivos trust acknowledged by a notary. As an extra precaution, the settlor may wish to initial each page of the inter vivos trust. Witnesses are not necessary to execute an inter vivos trust.

You may execute more than one original inter vivos trust. Execute the duplicates at the same time as the original.

Keeping Your Will Safe

Do not place the original will in a location where a person who would benefit if the will was *not* found after your death has access to it. Generally, a safe-deposit box is a good location for the original will, so long as any co-renter of the box has no interest in the will being destroyed. Having the safe-deposit box in your name only does not cause a delay in obtaining the original will. In most states, in the event of the death of the safe-deposit box renter, his or her safe-deposit box may be opened for the purpose of the will search. The box opening is done in the presence of a bank officer, who will make a copy of the will for the bank's file and give the original to the named executor in the will.

Some states permit you to file your original will with the clerk of the probate court before death. If this option appeals to you, call your local probate court clerk to see if your state permits such safekeeping and if your local probate court will be the custodian. Be sure to keep the *receipt* for the safekeeping of your will in a safe place, like your safe-deposit box.

Keeping Your Inter Vivos Trust Safe

Loss of your inter vivos trust during your lifetime could be a substantial problem, as you will likely transfer ownership of your estate to the name of the trust. If you do lose your inter vivos trust during your lifetime, it is imperative that you then *restate* the terms of your inter vivos trust with a *trust amendment.*

Generally, a safe-deposit box is a good location for the original inter vivos trust. It is a good idea that the safe-deposit box be held in the name of the inter vivos trust, so that successor trustees can remove assets in the safe-deposit box in the event of your death or incapacity. If your state law will not permit a safe-deposit box to be in the name of the inter vivos trust, consider placing a successor trustee or a co-trustee on the safe-deposit box as a co-renter of the box.

If you decide to keep the safe-deposit box in your name only, then at your death (but not incapacity) the successor trustee should be able to obtain the original inter vivos trust. In most states, in the event of the death of a safe-deposit box renter, his or her safe-deposit box may be opened for the purpose of an inter vivos trust search. The box opening is done in the presence of a bank officer, who will make a copy of the inter vivos trust for the bank's file and give the original to the named trustee in the inter vivos trust.

Revocation

You can revoke a will or inter vivos trust in two basic ways. First, you can revoke the will or inter vivos trust by physically destroying it or by crossing out all of the provisions of the will or inter vivos trust. However, revocation by destruction is not suggested, as a court might later determine that your physically destroyed or crossed-out will or inter vivos trust was merely lost and permit the use of a copy of it.

The best way to revoke a will is by a executing a new will that states on its face that all prior wills are revoked. All of the forms in this book have the standard revocation of prior wills language in the introductory paragraph.

Unless the inter vivos trust provides otherwise, only the person who creates the inter vivos trust (the settlor) can revoke it. As in a will, often the best way to revoke an inter vivos trust is to amend it by a complete restatement of the terms of the inter vivos trust. If you wish to revoke you inter vivos trust, it is recommended that you physically destroy the original inter vivos trust and execute a separate REVOCATION OF TRUST. (see form 52 and form 53.) Before you revoke your trust, make certain that you transfer all property in the trust to be revoked to either your name or to the name of the new trust.

Chapter 8:

Changing Your Will or Inter Vivos Trust

This chapter will explain how you can make changes to your will or inter vivos trust before you execute it, or by preparing a separate amendment to your executed inter vivos trust or an amendment (called a *codicil*) to your executed will.

Changes before Execution

While reviewing your will or inter vivos trust, you may find a small error or change you wish to make before you sign it. For example, the specific cash bequest to your sister is listed as $1,000, and you want to leave her $2,000. The simplest way of correcting or changing your unexecuted will is to simply make a handwritten correction by crossing out the "$1,000" and handwriting in "$2,000" next to the crossed-out amount. This is called an *interlineation*.

There is always a danger in making a change to your will or inter vivos trust before you execute it. How is the court supposed to know if you made the change before or after you signed the will or inter vivos trust? Handwritten or typed changes *before* you sign the will or inter vivos trust are valid. Such changes *after* you sign are invalid.

Before executing your will or inter vivos trust, date and initial each change, and have each witness initial the changes *before* you execute the will or inter vivos trust. If the will or inter vivos trust is challenged, the likelihood of the court determining that your handwritten changes are valid is increased if initiated. As the forms on the accompanying CD require various fill-in-the-blanks, these fill-ins should not be initiated.

Changes after Execution

Often, you want to make changes to your will or inter vivos trust *after* it has been executed. Do *not* make such changes by crossing out certain parts of the document or by interlineations. This method is *not* valid, even if you date and initial the changes.

Changes to Your Will

After your will is executed, you have two choices if you want to make changes. First, execute a new will. This is the preferred method if the changes are substantial or if the change may later hurt someone's feelings if they find out.

Example: *You want to leave $100 instead of $100,000 to your niece. Consider a new will rather than amending your existing will so that your niece will not know about the prior, larger bequest.*

Second, you can execute a separate document amending your will. This might be appropriate if the change is relatively small.

Example: *You want to leave $1,000 to your niece, who does not receive anything under your existing will. Consider an amendment to your will.*

Amendments to your will are called *codicils*. A codicil adds to your will, subtracts from your will, or simply replaces portions of your existing will. However, a codicil leaves intact those portions of your will not removed or replaced.

Example: *Your will names your sister as executor. You execute a codicil naming your brother as alternative executor. Your sister, pursuant to the will, is still your first appointed executor.*

Codicils are executed in the same manner as wills. A sample **CODICIL** is located on the CD-ROM. (see form 33.)

Changes to Your Inter Vivos Trust

After your inter vivos trust is executed, you have two choices if you want to make changes. First, you can execute a separate document, called an *amendment*, to insert the changes to your inter vivos trust. This is especially appropriate if the change is relatively small.

Example: *You want to leave the $1,000 to your niece who does not receive anything under your inter vivos trust. Consider an amendment to your inter vivos trust.*

Second, you can amend your entire inter vivos trust by a new inter vivos trust, called a *restatement*. Trust amendments by a restatement are done for several reasons.

◆ The changes are substantial.

◆ The change may later hurt someone's feelings if they find out.

Example: *You want to leave $100 instead of $100,000 to your niece. Consider an amendment by a complete restatement of your inter vivos trust rather than amending your existing inter vivos trust, so that your niece will not know about the prior, larger bequest.*

◆ You have made several changes over the years, and the various amendments to your inter vivos trust have made review of the inter vivos trust difficult.

Example: *You are amending your inter vivos trust for the tenth time. You have a twenty-page inter vivos trust plus ten five-page amendments, for a total of seventy pages. To understand your inter vivos trust, one must read the inter vivos trust and then read each amendment to determine the current provisions of your inter vivos trust. At this point, it would be easier to restate all of the terms of the inter vivos trust in a single, eleventh amendment by a restatement of the entire inter vivos trust.*

An amendment to your inter vivos trust subtracts or simply replaces portions of your existing inter vivos trust, but an amendment leaves intact those portions of your inter vivos trust not removed or replaced.

Trust amendments are executed in the same matter as trusts. Forms 46 and 47 are two types of TRUST AMENDMENTS.

Chapter 9:

Anatomy of Your Will or Inter Vivos Trust

This chapter explains the format of the will and inter vivos trust forms in this book. Refer to these instructions and explanations as you complete your desired forms. Additional paragraphs not discussed either contain necessary legal information to make your will or inter vivos trust valid, or are specific to the form you are using. Review each paragraph of the form you are using. Complete any necessary requirements it may have.

Will

Your will should contain each of the following elements, as long as they apply to you (if you do not have minor children, you will not need a guardianship nomination clause).

Title

The title, "Last Will and Testament," identifies the document as a will.

Introductory Clause/Revocation of Prior Wills

This paragraph:

> ◆ identifies you as the testator of the will;
>
> ◆ declares your county and state of residence to assure the county court that it is the proper county of jurisdiction in the event your will needs to be probated after your death; and,

◆ revokes any and all of your prior wills and codicils. (All prior wills and codicils are expressly revoked because if your new will does not automatically revoke prior wills and codicils, each would have to be read together with your new will.)

Paragraph FIRST

This paragraph is a declaration of your marital status, and it names any predeceased spouse in order to assist your executor, who must advise the court of the same in the event of the probate of your will. The names and birth dates of your children advises the court if you have any children, as well as identifies if any children are minors. Also listed are the names of any predeceased children as well as the names and birth dates of any descendants of predeceased children. These statements assist the executor in giving the required written legal notice to all heirs if the will is filed with the court for probate after your death. The statement "I have no other children or issue of a predeceased child" advises the executor and the court that you have no other issue.

NOTE: Directive to Pay Debts: *A directive to the executor to pay all of your debts adds nothing to the validity or effect of the will. By law, debts must be paid after your death before the bequests are paid. Accordingly, this paragraph is NOT used in the forms included with this book.*

Paragraph SECOND

This paragraph directs the disposition of your property subject to your will. Most will forms in this book provide separately for bequests of personal property (both tangible and intangible), cash, real property, and the residue of your estate.

Paragraph THIRD

This paragraph provides comprehensive disinheritance and anti-contest clauses. The *disinheritance clause* states that all persons other than your specifically named beneficiaries are disinherited. If someone shows up after your death claiming to be your long-lost brother, he is still subject to the disinheritance clause and will receive no part of your estate.

The *anti-contest clause* disinherits anyone who contests the will. It also disinherits any persons who attempt to contest non-will transfers—such as joint tenancies, TOD securities accounts, or life insurance—or who make claims against your estate for services rendered or under alleged oral agreements to share property.

Paragraph FOURTH

This paragraph nominates the executor of the will and permits the executor to sell property without publishing a written notice of his or her intent to sell the property.

After Paragraph FOURTH is the subscription statement, where you date and sign your will.

Attestation Clause

After your signature is the attestation clause, where the witnesses declare under penalty of perjury that they witnessed your will. By making their statement under penalty of perjury, some states do not require their testimony to prove the validity of your will if its execution is not contested after you die. The will is considered self-proving. For a will to be considered self-proving in other states, you and your witnesses need to execute, in the presence of a notary, the SELF-PROVING AFFIDAVIT appropriate for your state found on the CD-ROM. At the end of the attestation clause, the witnesses will sign their names and someone will affix the date.

Guardianship Nomination

If you have minor children and you wish to nominate a guardian to raise them (or manage their estates if no custodian or trustee is named), you need to execute one of the two separate forms provided. (see form 1 and form 2.)

Inter Vivos Trust

Your inter vivos trust should contain all of the following elements.

Title

The title "INTER VIVOS TRUST" identifies the document as a revocable, amendable, living trust.

Article I

Paragraph 1.01. The introductory clause identifies you as the settlor or settlors, and identifies the persons who will act as your trustee (probably you) of your inter vivos trust. It also establishes the trust by your declaration and refers to the assets that you declare to be part of your inter vivos trust as "Exhibit A," which should be attached to the end of your inter vivos trust.

Paragraph 1.02. This paragraph identifies the name and date of your inter vivos trust. Although you can give your inter vivos trust any name you want, it is recommended that you use your own name.

Paragraph 1.03. Here, you define certain terms used in your inter vivos trust.

Paragraph 1.04 (married couple's inter vivos trust). This paragraph confirms that separate property of either spouse or community property contributed to your inter vivos trust remains the separate property of the contributing spouse or the couple's community property.

Article II

Paragraphs 2.01 and 2.02. These paragraphs provide that during your lifetime (if your inter vivos trust is created by only you) or during the joint lifetime of you and your spouse, all of the trust income and that principal are requested to be paid to you or both of you.

Paragraph 2.03. This paragraph provides that in the event of your incapacity or your spouse's incapacity (if your inter vivos trust was created by you and your spouse), the trustee shall make appropriate payments from the trust income and principal for your support. If you have a single-person inter vivos trust, then the trustee is instructed to make payments during your incapacity at a level that would permit you to remain in your home, even if it requires twenty-four-hour care and exhausts the principal of the trust. (This instruction is not given in the married couple's inter vivos trust form, as the non-incapacitated spouse should have greater flexibility in determining how the total estate is expended for the benefit of the incapacitated spouse.)

Paragraphs 2.04 and 2.05. These paragraphs provide that you, as a single settlor, may revoke or amend your inter vivos trust at any time. It also provides that you and your spouse, as married settlors of a joint inter vivos trust, may only revoke or amend as to community property jointly, but that each of you may amend or revoke the inter vivos trust as to your separate property.

Article III

Paragraph 3.01. Here, you direct the trustee to pay the debts of the deceased settlor. If you have a married couple's inter vivos trust form, this paragraph also gives the surviving spouse all of the inter vivos trust estate.

Paragraph 3.02. If you have a single person inter vivos trust, this paragraph directs the disposition of your assets that are subject to your inter vivos trust at your death. If you have a married couple's inter vivos trust, this paragraph directs the disposition of your assets that are subject to your inter vivos trust at the death of the surviving spouse. The inter vivos trust forms in this book provide for bequests of intangible personal property, cash, real property, and the residue of your inter vivos trust estate. Tangible personal property is bequeathed in the pourover will that you will execute in addition to the your inter vivos trust.

If you have a married couple's inter vivos trust, this paragraph either creates a decedent's trust and survivor's trust out of your inter vivos trust on the death of the predeceasing spouse, or a decedent's trust, a marital trust, and survivor's trust out of your inter vivos trust on the death of the predeceasing spouse.

In form 40 and form 45, the survivor's trust consists of the surviving spouse's one-half interest in any community property in the inter vivos trust, *plus* the surviving spouse's separate property in the inter vivos trust, *plus* whatever the predeceasing spouse did not leave to the decedent's trust. In form 41 and form 42, the survivor's trust consists of the surviving spouse's one-half interest in any community property in the inter vivos trust *plus* the surviving spouse's separate property in the inter vivos trust.

In those forms, the decedent's trust is funded with assets from the predeceasing spouse's separate property in the inter vivos trust or the predeceasing spouse's one-half interest in community property in the inter vivos trust that has a value equal to the federal estate tax exemption available in the predeceasing spouse's year of death. (For 2007, that amount is $2,000,000.)

In form 44, the marital trust is funded with assets from the predeceasing spouse's separate property in the inter vivos trust or the predeceasing spouse's one-half interest in community property in the inter vivos trust that were not funded into the decedent's trust. (In other words, the amount of the predeceasing spouse's estate in excess of the federal estate tax exemption amount.)

After the death of the predeceasing spouse, the decedent's trust and marital trust become irrevocable and not amendable. However, the surviving spouse continues to have the power to amend or revoke the survivor's trust.

Further, the surviving spouse is entitled to any part of the principal of the survivor's trust plus 5% of the principal, annually (if he or she wants), from the marital trust. Finally, the surviving spouse is entitled to principal from the decedent's trust or marital trust if necessary for his or her care or support, in his or her accustomed manner of living.

Paragraph 3.03 (only in married couple's inter vivos trust forms). Here, you direct the trustee to pay the debts of the surviving spouse upon your death.

Paragraph 3.04 (only in married couple's inter vivos trust forms). This paragraph permits the surviving spouse to direct the distribution of the survivor's trust by a written document called a *testamentary power of appointment* to whomever he or she wishes. However, absent such a written directive, the survivor's trust shall be distributed in the same manner as the decedent's trust and marital trust as directed in Paragraph 3.05.

Paragraph 3.05 (only in married couple's inter vivos trust forms). This paragraph directs the disposition of the decedent's trust and marital trust. This disposition plan became irrevocable at the death of the predeceasing spouse. The inter vivos trust forms in this book provide for bequests of intangible personal property, cash, real property, and the residue of your inter vivos trust estate. However, it does not provide for tangible, personal property, as it is bequeathed in the *pourover will* that you will execute in addition to the your inter vivos trust.

Article IV

Paragraph 4.01. This paragraph confirms who is the original trustee and provides for succession of successor trustees. The forms provide that the settlors will be the original trustees. However, you can change those defaults. If a settlor who is acting as a trustee becomes incapacitated, his or her restoration to capacity shall restore him or her as a trustee. In married couple inter vivos trust forms, a *special* trustee shall be appointed to hold any life insurance policy on the life of the surviving spouse that is held as an asset of the decedent's trust.

Paragraph 4.02. In the single person inter vivos trusts, you may change the order of trustee succession at any time. In the married persons' trusts, the change of trustee succession must be done jointly if both spouses are living, or by the surviving spouse alone.

Paragraph 4.06. This paragraph lists the expansive powers of the trustees in terms of management and investment of the trust estate. The range of powers that can be granted or withheld from a trustee is too vast to completely discuss here. The powers given are designed to permit a trustee to act within the general statutory guidelines allowed by most states.

Paragraph 4.06K. This paragraph is for married couples' inter vivos trusts only. It is designed to avoid the problem of needing the trustees (i.e., husband and wife) to act jointly to transact bank and stock brokerage transactions of check writing and securities trading.

Article V

Paragraph 5.01. This paragraph prohibits a beneficiary of an irrevocable portion of the inter vivos trust (i.e., the beneficiaries after the death of the original settlor or settlors or the surviving spouse as to a decedent's trust or marital trust) from assigning his or her share to another. It further prohibits the creditors of such beneficiary from attaching the beneficiary's interest in the trust.

Paragraph 5.02. Here, you provide for the trustee to use the *Uniform Principal and Income Act* to allocate expenses and income between principal and income. For example, under trust law, a capital gain on a sale or disposition is considered a principal receipt and not distributed to an ordinary *income* beneficiary.

Paragraph 5.03. This paragraph provides that the trust will have to end in about ninety years so it does not violate the common law doctrine of *rule against perpetuities* (i.e., that a trust cannot last forever). Approximately eleven states have abolished the rule against perpetuities, so in those states, a trust can last forever.

Paragraph 5.04. This paragraph permits the trustee to make payments to a beneficiary or the beneficiary's guardian or even to make payments for the benefit of a beneficiary directly (e.g., pay the beneficiary's house payment directly).

Paragraph 5.08. Here, you provide for the ultimate disposition of the trust if all named beneficiaries are deceased. If you have a single-person trust, then it all goes to your heirs. If you have a married couple's trust, then one-half goes to the heirs of each spouse. You can provide for a different disposition of your assets if you wish.

Paragraph 5.16. This paragraph provides for which state law is to be used in construing the trust. Normally, you list your home state.

Paragraph 5.17. This paragraph provides a comprehensive disinheritance and anti-contest clauses. The *disinheritance clause* states that all persons other than your specifically named beneficiaries are disinherited. If someone shows up after your death claiming to be your long-lost brother, he is still subject to the disinheritance clause and receives no part of your estate.

The *anti-contest clause* disinherits anyone who contests your inter vivos trust, as well as persons who attempt to contest other date of death transfers—such as joint tenancies, TOD securities accounts, or life insurance—or who make claims against your estate for services rendered or under alleged oral agreements to share property.

Paragraph 5.18. This paragraph provides that a beneficiary must survive you or your spouse (as the case may be) by thirty days to be entitled to his or her bequest under the trust.

Paragraph 5.19. This paragraph provides that all typed and handwritten *fill-ins,* where directed, in your inter vivos trust were made before the execution of your trust and are not initialed by you. All crossed-through words and interlineations were made before the execution of your trust and are initialed by you.

After Paragraph 5.19 is the *Certification,* where you date and sign your inter vivos trust in the presence of a notary, who acknowledges your signature.

"Exhibit A" is a list of the assets you declare to be part of your inter vivos trust. However, a simple declaration such as Exhibit A, even if in writing, is usually insufficient to actually transfer the asset to your inter vivos trust. You must physically change the title of the assets that you want to transfer to your inter vivos trust. (see Chapter 8.)

Conclusion

As previously stated, estate planning is an essential activity for every individual or couple. By reading this book and using the forms provided, you are now ready to put into action a plan that will protect your assets, provide for your minor children, and avoid paying exorbitant federal estate taxes. With some thoughtful analysis, careful drafting and execution, and the all important follow-through of funding, you can have peace of mind and know that you will be transferring maximum wealth at your death. By reviewing the samples and selecting the most appropriate form for your situation, you can accomplish your goals.

Glossary

A

administrator. A personal representative who is not named in the decedent's will. In earlier times, a female administrator was called an administratrix. *See also executor and personal representative.*

anti-contest clause. A clause that disinherits anyone who contests the will. It also disinherits any persons who attempt to contest non-will transfers, such as joint tenancies, TOD securities accounts, or life insurance, or anyone who make claims against your estate for services rendered or under alleged oral agreements to share property.

attestation clause. The clause after your signature where the witnesses declare under penalty of perjury that they witnessed your will.

B

beneficiary. The named recipient of an asset belonging to a decedent. *See also heir.*

bequest. A gift effective at time of death.

bond. An insurance policy issued to provide financial protection to an estate, a trust, or a custodianship from the dishonest acts of a fiduciary (i.e., an executor, trustee, or custodian).

C

certification. Where you date and sign your inter vivos trust in the presence of a notary who acknowledges your signature.

codicil. An amendment to a will.

community property. Property acquired during marriage from the efforts of one or more of the spouses. Term applies in Arizona, California, Idaho, Louisiana, Nevada, New Mexico, Texas, Washington, and Wisconsin. *See also separate property.*

custodian. A person appointed under the *Uniform Gift to Minors Act* (sometimes called *Uniform Transfers to Minors Act*), who has a fiduciary position over assets that are for the benefit of a minor or person under the age of 25 years. In essence, a trustee without formal trust documents.

D

decedent. A person who has died.

decedent's trust. A trust created at the decedent's death to take advantage of the decedent's federal estate tax exemption.

descendant. A living person born into the family line (a child, grandchild, etc.).

devise. Generally, a bequest of real property. In many states, used interchangeably with "bequest."

devisee. The person who is left real property in a will.

disinheritance clause. The clause that states that all persons other than your specifically named beneficiaries are disinherited.

disqualified person. California is the only state to currently have a disqualified persons statute. If bequests you are considering fall within the California disqualified persons statute, you should consider safeguards such as qualifying procedures. It is important to be aware of such laws, as they can, if enacted, apply retroactively.

E

elective share. *See forced share.*

executor. A personal representative who is named in the decedent's will. In earlier times, a female executor was called an executrix. *See also administrator and personal representative.*

execution. The act of signing a will by the testator and the witnesses.

exemption trust. *See decedent's trust.*

F

family allowance. An amount allowed by statute to go to the spouse and children of decedent.

fiduciary. A term describing a duty to act on behalf of or for another in a fair and trustworthy manner. Also used to describe a person who holds such a duty.

forced share. Rights granted by state law to the surviving spouse to take a portion of the decedent's estate regardless of what the will allows.

G

grantor. *See settlor.*

guardian. Person appointed to care for the person and/or estate of a minor.

H

heir. The relative entitled to an asset belonging to a decedent when no person is named as the beneficiary. *See also beneficiary.*

holographic will. A will wherein the essential terms are all in the handwriting of the testator. Although the will must be signed by the testator, the signature need not be at the end of the document, and the will need not be witnessed by any other persons. This type of will is valid in most states.

I

interlineations. When one or more words are inserted between the lines or on the margin of a document, such as a will.

inter vivos trust. A trust created during lifetime (instead of created at someone's death via their will). Generally, the trust is for the benefit of the person who creates the trust, but it becomes irrevocable upon the death of the person who creates the trust. *See also living trust.*

intestate. When a person dies without a will.

intestate succession. The distribution of a decedent's property to the decedent's heirs when there is either no will or the will fails to dispose of the property.

in trust for (I/T/F). A way to designate that certain assets are being held in trust for another person.

I.R.C. 529 College Plan.   State-run college education programs permitted by the Internal Revenue Code, wherein accounts can be funded by persons for the higher educational benefit of others they select. These programs have substantial federal income tax advantages when the account assets are used for higher educational expenses.

issue.   Legal term to describe the lineal descendants of a person. Your issue would be your children, your grandchildren, your great-grandchildren, and so on.

J

joint tenancy.   A written title naming one or more persons as joint tenants, which means they have equal ownership. In the event of the death of a joint tenant, the remaining joint tenants take the share of the deceased joint tenant by right of survivorship, regardless of contrary provisions in a will.

L

legacy.   A gift of personal property in a will.

life estate.   The right to use property during a person's lifetime, but not the right to dispose of the entire property during life or any of the property at death. *See also inter vivos trust.*

living trust.   A trust created during a person's lifetime (instead of created at someone's death via their will). Generally, the trust is for the benefit of the person who creates the trust, but it becomes irrevocable upon the death of the person who creates the trust. *See also inter vivos trust.*

M

marital property. Property acquired during marriage from the efforts of one or more of the spouses. *See also separate property.*

marital trust. A trust, created at death, of a decedent's assets for the benefit of the decedent's spouse that takes advantage of federal estate tax exemptions, but is not able to be changed by the surviving spouse.

married couple's trust. As used in this book, when a couple creates a joint trust, to which each person contributes assets.

minor. In most states, someone under the age of 18 years.

N

notary. A person authorized to administer oaths.

P

payable on death (POD). An account that passes directly to a designated beneficiary upon the owner's death.

personal property. Anything that is not real property; for example, cash, securities, partnership interests, rights in a lawsuit, household furniture and furnishings, and personal effects.

personal representative. The generic term for the court-appointed person or corporation who manages a decedent's probate estate.

power of appointment. The right to direct in writing the disposition of assets.

probate. The court supervision of the changing of titles to assets from a decedent's name to the name of the beneficiaries under the decedent's will, or to the decedent's heirs if the decedent died with no will.

probate code. Statutes enacted in virtually every state that govern wills, trusts, and probate.

Q

quasi-community property. Property acquired by a married person who dies a resident of a community property state, while owning property acquired while he or she was living outside of the community property state. At the time of death, that property must have been community property if the person had been living in the community property state at the time the property was acquired. In such a situation, the quasi-community property is treated like community property.

R

real property. Land, buildings on land, long-term leases, mineral rights, condominiums, and co-op buildings (condos where the ownership is indicated by a certificate rather than a deed).

remainder. Balance of an estate after all specific gifts have been distributed.

remainderman. Person who takes the property after the life usage of the property by another. For example, if the testator bequeaths a life estate in his residence to Bob, and then at Bob's death the residence passes to Mary, then Mary is the *remainderman.*

residue. Those assets of an estate or a will that are left over after the distribution of all specific bequests.

restatement. This involves restating the terms of the inter vivos trust and acts as an amendment as a way to revoke the trust.

right of representation.   To take the place, for inheritance purposes, of a deceased ancestor. For example, if a will leaves a testator's estate to "my issue by right of representation," and the testator leaves two living children and one deceased child who left two children of his or her own, then the estate would go one-third to each of the living children of the testator and one-sixth to each of the children of the deceased child of the testator.

S

self-proving affidavit. A document used in most states so that a witness will not be needed to testify in court to prove a will offered for probate is the last will of testament of the decedent.

self-proving will. If a will is self-proving under the law of a particular state, nearly all states will permit the admission to probate of uncontested wills without testimony of a witness to the will. In California, a will is self-proving if the witnesses attest, under penalty of perjury, that the will was properly executed.

separate property. Property that belongs entirely to one person.

settlor. The person creating a trust.

subscribed will. A will that is signed by the testator at the end of the document and then signed by at least two witnesses.

successor trustee. A person or entity (e.g., bank trust department) that serves as trustee of a trust document upon the resignation, removal, or death of a trustee. For most inter vivos trusts, this is the person or entity named to act as trustee once the original trustee is no longer able to do so.

surety bond. An inexpensive form of insurance to guarantee that the executor will act honestly. A surety bond posted by the executor is in an amount equal to the value of the personal property of estate (real property does not have to be bonded, as it cannot be sold without consent of the beneficiaries or the court).

survivor's trust. A trust created at death for the benefit of the decedent's spouse that takes advantage of federal estate tax exemptions, and the surviving spouse has the power to make changes to it.

T

tax credit trust. *See decedent's trust.*

testamentary capacity. The legal and mental capacity to execute a will. Generally defined as being 18 years of age or older and aware of one's assets and relatives, and knowledge that the document takes effect at time of death.

testamentary trust. A trust created by a person's will, effective only upon the death of the testator.

testate. When a person dies with a will.

testator. The person whose will is being discussed.

Totten trust. Assets designated "in trust for" another person.

transfer on death (TOD). An account that passes directly to a designated beneficiary upon the owner's death.

trust. A legal entity and relationship wherein one person or entity holds legal title and responsibility to property for the financial benefit of another person or entity.

trustee. Person who holds title to the trust assets for the benefit of the beneficiary of the trust. A trustee is responsible for managing the trust assets and has a fiduciary relationship to the beneficiaries of the trust.

trustor. *See settlor.*

W

will. A document that, at someone's death, directs the distribution of his or her assets. A will generally cannot affect the distribution of assets held in joint tenancy, distributed pursuant to a contract (life insurance, pensions, retirement plans, annuities, etc.), or property subject to a payable on death or transfer on death designation.

witness. A person who sees a testator sign his or her will and signs the will after the testator. A witness must be 18 years or older, aware that the document he or she is signing is a will, and not a beneficiary under the will who takes any more than he or she would have under intestate succession.

Appendix A:

Forced Share Statutes

Virtually every state permits a surviving spouse, regardless of the terms of the decedent's will, to claim a certain portion of the decedent's estate. Some states call this a *forced share* or *elective share,* as the decedent's estate is forced to leave a certain portion to the surviving spouse or the surviving spouse can elect to take a certain portion.

The forced share is sometimes independent of a surviving spouse's right to other probate protections, such as *family allowance* (often called a *widow's allowance*). A family allowance is the right for a surviving spouse and minor children to receive a monthly stipend from the estate during probate administration. The right often includes the ability to stay in the family residence and retain certain personal property, such as household furniture. Other items may be specifically included by statute in the family allowance, regardless of the terms of the will.

In some states, the forced share only affects property that is disposed of by will or intestate succession. This means that property passing by joint tenancy, inter vivos trust, or contract (e.g., pensions and life insurance) is not affected. Some states look at the assets of the surviving spouse and the length of the marriage in determining the amount of the forced share for the surviving spouse. Nearly all states permit the surviving spouse to waive his or her right to the forced share either before or after the death of the decedent.

Following is a very brief summary of each state's forced share rules. As many factors particular to each state affect the application of the rules, it is wise to review the state's *actual* statute. You can find the statutes in your local law library or by doing an online search.

Summary of Forced Share Rules

Alabama: The surviving spouse is entitled to the lesser of one-third of the decedent spouse's estate or all of the decedent spouse's estate reduced by the value of the surviving spouse's separate property.
(Ala. Code Sec. 43-8-70 through 43-8-76.)

Alaska: The surviving spouse is entitled to one-third of the estate after payment of funeral expenses, family allowances, administration expenses, and certain claims.
(Alaska Stat. Sec. 13.12.202.)

Arizona: No forced share rights. However, because Arizona is a community property state, the surviving spouse owns one-half of the community property. Surviving spouse has rights to family allowances.
(Ariz. Rev. Stat. Ann. Sec. 14-2101 through 14-2114.)

Arkansas: Depending on the length of the marriage, number of children, and whether the real estate is ancestral, the surviving spouse can elect to take a life estate in one-third to one-half of the real property in the decedent's estate and between one-third and one-half of the personal property of the decedent's estate.
(Ark. Code Ann. Secs. 28-11-307, 28-39-201, and 28-39-401.)

California: No forced share rights. However, as California is a community property state, the surviving spouse owns one-half of the community property and one-half of quasi-community property.
(Cal. Probate Code Sec. 6401, 6560 and 6561.)

Colorado: The surviving spouse is entitled to up to one-half of the estate, depending on the years of the marriage.
(Colo. Rev. Stat. Sec. 15-11-201 through 15-11-208.)

Connecticut: The surviving spouse is entitled to use one-third of the estate for his or her lifetime.
(Conn. Gen. Stat. Ann. Sec. 45a-436.)

Delaware: The surviving spouse is entitled to take one-third of the estate less what he or she received otherwise as a result of the decedent's death.
(Del. Code Ann. Title 12 Sec. 19-101.)

District of Columbia: The surviving spouse can elect to receive, depending on who survives the decedent, one-third to one-half of the decedent's estate.
(D.C. Stat. Ann. Sec. 19-113 and 19-302 through 19-304.)

Florida: The surviving spouse can take elect to take 30% of the estate (except for real property outside of Florida). The surviving spouse also has the right to certain household items, personal effects, and one car.
(Fla. State. Ann. Sec. 732.201 through 732.2155.)

Georgia: The surviving spouse is entitled to one year's support.
(Ga. Code Ann. Sec. 53-3-5.)

Hawaii: Depending on the length of the marriage, the surviving spouse can take up to one-half of the decedent's estate or $50,000, whichever amount is greater.
(Haw. Rev. Stat. Sec. 560:2-201 through 2-207.)

Idaho: As Idaho is a community property state, the surviving spouse owns one-half of the community property. The surviving spouse can elect to take one-half of quasi-community property. In addition, the surviving spouse can keep all benefits under the decedent's will.
(Idaho Code Sec. 15-2-201 through 15-2-206.)

Illinois: If there is no surviving issue of the decedent, the surviving spouse can elect to take one-half of the estate. If there are descendants of the decedent, the surviving spouse can elect to take one-third of the estate.
(755 ILCS 5/2-8.)

Indiana: If there are no surviving issue of the decedent from a prior marriage, the surviving spouse can elect to take one-half of the estate. If there are descendants of the decedent from a prior marriage, the surviving spouse can elect to take an amount equal to one-third of the personal property and one-fourth of the real property.
(Ind. Code Ann. Sec. 29-1-3-1.)

Iowa: The surviving spouse can elect to take all of the personal property and one-half of the real property of the decedent.
(Iowa Code Ann. Sec. 633-230.)

Kansas: Depending on the length of the marriage, the surviving spouse can take up to one-half of the decedent's estate or $50,000, whichever amount is greater.
(Kan. Stat. Ann. Sec. 59-6A201 through 59-6A211.)

Kentucky: The surviving spouse can elect to take one-third of the value of the real estate and one-half of the value of the personal property in the decedent's estate.
(Ky. Rev. Stat. Ann. Sec. 392.080.)

Louisiana: As Louisiana is a community property state, the surviving spouse owns one-half of the community property. Further, the surviving spouse can claim a *legal usufruct for life,* which is similar to a life estate (unless he or she remarries), over a portion of the decedent's estate.
(La. Civ. Code Ann. Art. 890.)

Maine: The surviving spouse can elect to take one-third of the augmented estate.
(Me. Rev. Stat. Ann. Tit. 18A, Sec. 2-201 through 2-207.)

Maryland: The surviving spouse can elect to take one-third of the estate if there are children or one-half of the estate if there are no children. (Md. Code Ann. Est. & Trust, Sec. 3-203 through 3-208.)

Massachusetts: The surviving spouse can elect to take the first $25,000 plus the income/life estate of one-third of the estate if there are children, or the first $25,000 plus the income/life estate of one-half of the estate if there are no children. (Mass. Gen Laws Ann. Ch. 191 Sec. 15.)

Michigan: The surviving spouse can elect to take one-half of his or her intestate share, reduced by one-half of the value of all other property passing to the surviving spouse by the decedent by means outside of the will. In intestate succession, the surviving spouse takes 100% if there are no issue or parents of the decedent, and takes the first $150,000 plus one-half if there are issue of the decedent. (Mich. Comp. Laws Ann. Sec. 700-2102 and 700-2202.)

Minnesota: Depending on the length of the marriage, the surviving spouse can take up to one-half of the decedent's estate or $50,000, whichever amount is greater. (Minn. Stat. Ann. Sec. 524.2-201 through 524.2-214.)

Mississippi: The surviving spouse can elect against the will and take his or her intestate share, which is no greater than one-half. (Miss. Code Ann. Sec. 91-5-25.)

Missouri: The surviving spouse can elect to take one-third of the estate if there are children or one-half of the estate if there are no children. (Mo. Rev. Stat. Sec. 474.160.)

Montana: Depending on the length of the marriage, the surviving spouse can take up to one-half of the decedent's estate or $50,000, whichever amount is greater. (Mont. Code Ann. Sec. 72-2-221 through 72-2-230.)

Nebraska: The surviving spouse is entitled to take up to one-half of the estate. (Neb. Rev. Stat. Sec. 30-2313 through 30-2319.)

Nevada: No forced share rights. However, as Nevada is a community property state, the surviving spouse owns one-half of the community property. Nevada also provides that a spouse who is not named in the will is, in most cases, entitled to between one-third and one-half of the decedent's spouse's estate. (Nev. Rev. Stat. Sec. 134.040 through 134.050.)

New Hampshire: The surviving spouse is entitled to take between one-third and one-half of the estate. (N.H. Rev. Stat. Ann. Sec. 560.10.)

New Jersey: The surviving spouse is entitled to take up to one-third of the estate. (N.J. Stat. Ann. Sec. 3B:8-10.)

New Mexico: No forced share rights. However, as New Mexico is a community property state, the surviving spouse owns one-half of the community property. (N.M. Stat. Ann. Sec. 45-2-301.)

New York: The surviving spouse may elect to take his or her intestate share, between one-third and one-half of the decedent's estate. (N.Y. Probate Law Sec. 5-1.1.)

North Carolina: The surviving spouse is entitled to take between one-sixth and one-half of the estate, depending on what issue survived the decedent. (N.C. Gen Stat. Sec. 30-3-1.)

North Dakota: The surviving spouse is entitled to take up to one-half of the estate, depending on the years of the marriage. (N.D. Cent Code Sec. 30.1-05 through 30.1-08.)

Ohio: The surviving spouse may elect to take his or her intestate share up to $60,000, plus between one-third and one-half of the decedent's estate. (Ohio Rev. Code Ann. Sec. 2106.01.)

Oklahoma: The surviving spouse may elect to take one-half of the property acquired during the marriage by the joint industry of the spouses, plus a conditional life estate in a homestead.
(Okla. Stat. Title. Sec. 84-44.)

Oregon: The surviving spouse can elect to take one-fourth reduced by the value of all other property passing to the surviving spouse by the decedent.
(Or. Rev. Stat. Sec. 114.105.)

Pennsylvania: The surviving spouse is entitled to take one-third of the estate.
(Pa. Stat. Ann. Title 20, Sec. 2203-2211.)

Rhode Island: Besides the provisions by the decedent's will to a surviving spouse, the surviving spouse is also entitled to a life estate in all real property.
(R.I. Gen. Laws Sec. 33-25-2 through 33-25-6.)

South Carolina: The surviving spouse is entitled to take one-third of the estate.
(S.C. Code Ann. Sec. 62-2-201 through 62-2-207.)

South Dakota: Depending on the length of the marriage, the surviving spouse can take up to one-half of the decedent's estate or $50,000, whichever amount is greater.
(S.D. Codified Laws Ann. Sec. 29A-2-201 through 29A-2-214.)

Tennessee: Depending on the length of the marriage, the surviving spouse can take up to 40% of the decedent's estate.
(Tenn. Code Ann. Sec. 31-4-101,102.)

Texas: No forced share rights. However, as Texas is a community property state, the surviving spouse owns one-half of the community property.
(Texas Statutes, Probate Code Sec. 45.)

Utah: The surviving spouse is entitled to take one-third of the estate of the decedent or $25,000, whichever amount is greater.
(Utah Code Ann. Sec. 75-2-201 through 75-2-207.)

Vermont: The surviving spouse is entitled to take at least one-third of the estate. (Vt. Stat. Ann. Title 14, Sec. 401.)

Virginia: The surviving spouse is entitled to take between one-third and one-half of the estate, depending on what issue survived the decedent. (Va. Code Ann. Sec. 64.16.)

Washington: No forced share rights. However, as Washington is a community property state, the surviving spouse owns one-half of the community property. (Wash. Rev. Code Ann. Secs. 11.04.015 and 11.12.095.)

West Virginia: The surviving spouse is entitled to take up to one-half of the estate, depending on the years of the marriage. (W. Va. Code Sec. 42-3-1 through 42-3-7.)

Wisconsin: The surviving spouse is entitled to take one-half of the estate. (Wis. Stat. Ann. Chapter 861.02.)

Wyoming: The surviving spouse is entitled to take between one-fourth and one-half of the estate, depending on what issue survived the decedent. (Wyo. Stat. Title 2, Chapter 5, Sec. 101.)

Appendix B:

Asset Roadmap

Sometimes no one—not even the decedent's family—has any idea what the assets of the estate are, or where they should look for the decedent's will and other important papers. In those cases, the family find health care powers of attorney after the decedent has died or the decedent's burial instructions after the funeral—when it is too late. To avoid putting your family through such heartache, keep an *asset roadmap,* detailing where your important papers can be found and listing both your assets and the tentative disposition of your assets that pass outside of your will and probate.

The following roadmap should be copied and used by you, from time to time, to update where your family can find your will, inter vivos trust, powers of attorney for health care and estate management, safe-deposit box, as well as a listing of your life, health, car, and home insurance. If you want, you can even list where you keep your tax returns and make a suggestion as to what attorney your family should hire to assist them in the event of your death. In addition, there is space to insert, right on the roadmap, a legally binding directive as to your burial or funeral instructions. Finally, the roadmap permits you to list your assets—your real property, securities, bank accounts, and any other assets you own.

Instructions

Will. List the date of your will, where the original is kept, and who the nominated executor is.

Trust. List the date of your inter vivos trust, where the original is kept, and who the successor trustees are.

Codicil. List the date of your codicil and where the original is kept.

Powers of Attorney. List the date, location of the original, and name of the nominated agent for both your health care power of attorney and your power of attorney for estate management. (Remember, by law, a copy of your health care power of attorney has the legal effect of an original.)

Safe-Deposit Box. List the name and location of the bank, the location of the safe-deposit box key, the number of the box, and the names of any co-renters of the box.

Life Insurance. List the name of each insurance company, the face amount of the policy, the policy number, the location of the original policy, and the name of the policy beneficiary.

Other Insurance. List the location of your original policies for your car, home, etc.

Burial/Funeral Instructions. You may leave written instructions as to the disposition of your remains. If you have made prearrangements, or if you own a crypt or plot, include that information as well as the location of any pre-need contracts or cemetery deeds.

Assets. List all of your real property, securities, bank accounts, personal property (such as cars and boats), and other miscellaneous property.

Real Property. List the location of the property and how you hold title. For example, "20 Maple Street, Los Angeles, John Smith and Mary Smith, as joint tenants."

Securities. List all stocks, bonds, and brokerage accounts. As to actual certificates for stocks and bonds, you should list the number of shares under the subheading "Account #." For brokerage accounts, you do not need to list the individual securities within the account. As with real property, list how the title is held as to each security or brokerage account. If you hold a brokerage account in your name with a transfer on death designation, list your name with TOD and the name of the beneficiary in the event of your death.

Bank Accounts. List the name and location of each financial institution, the account numbers, where the bank books or CD certificates are located, and the title vesting for each account. For Totten trust accounts, list your name, then ATF ("as trustee for"), and then the name of the beneficiary in the event of your death.

Autos/Boats/Etc. List the location of the certificate of title for each asset. The certificate of title itself will indicate any co-ownership rights.

Partnerships/Annuities/Royalties/Misc. Assets. List the names of assets, location of original documentation of ownership, a description of the assets with any account number, and the name of any beneficiary.

Tax Returns. List where your prior year tax returns can be found.

Lawyer Referral. List the name of any lawyer that has information concerning any of the above, or who you would like your family or beneficiaries to contact regarding assistance in the handling of your estate.

ASSET ROADMAP

WILL	
Date	
Location	
Executor	

TRUST	
Date	
Location	
Successor Trustee	

CODICIL	
Date	
Location	

POWERS OF ATTORNEY	
HEALTH	
Date	
Location	
Agent	
FINANCIAL (ESTATE MANAGEMENT)	
Date	
Location	
Agent	

SAFE-DEPOSIT BOX	
Location	
Location of Key	
Box #	
Co-Renter	

LIFE INSURANCE

Company

Amount

Policy #

Location

Company

Amount

Policy #

Location

Company

Amount

Policy #

Location

Company

Amount

Policy #

Location

OTHER INSURANCE

Auto

Household

Other

BURIAL/FUNERAL INSTRUCTIONS

ASSETS

REAL PROPERTY

Location

Title

Location

Title

Location

Title

Location

Title

SECURITIES

Name   Account #

Title

1.

2.

3.

4.

5.

BANK ACCOUNTS

Location   Account #

Title

1.

2.

3.

4.

5.

AUTOS/BOATS/ETC.

Description of Auto/Boat/etc.

Location of Title Certificate

Description of Auto/Boat/etc.

Location of Title Certificate

Description of Auto/Boat/etc.

Location of Title Certificate

PARTNERSHIPS/ANNUITIES/ROYALTIES/MISC. ASSETS

1.

2.

3.

TAX RETURNS

Location

LAWYER REFERRAL

Appendix C:

Step-by-Step Instructions with Sample, Completed Forms

This appendix contains detailed instructions for filling out the forms, as well as many filled-in sample forms. Following are some things to keep in mind while filling out your own estate planning documents.

An individual would create an inter vivos trust wherein he or she was the sole settlor (the person creating the trust). The individual can be single or married. The trust forms in this book and the CD-ROM call such a trust a *single person trust*. Other trust forms in this book and its CD-ROM are referred to as married couples' trusts. A *married couple's trust* is one with two or more settlors. Often, the married couple's trust is created by a married couple, but it can be created by two or more persons who are not married (e.g., domestic partners, siblings, or friends). However, only married couples can utilize the concept of the *marital deduction* referred to in several of the forms on the CD-ROM.

For each section in which you bequeath any kind of property to any individual, institution, or trust, write "end of list" after you have listed the name of the recipient. This will keep dishonest people from adding their names to the list and trying to take part of your estate. You will see this tactic used in some of the sample forms.

Note that the executions provided in the sample forms and on the blank forms on the CD-ROM will not work for every state. The *execution* is the part of the document wherein you sign and print your name, date it, and get it notarized. Check with your state to be sure you use the proper form of execution for your estate planning documents.

Number Key

In the forms included in this book, the blanks to be filled in by you are each numbered. Use the following as a reference guide on how to complete each blank based upon its assigned number. (Three sample, completed forms are located in this section. Use these as models to complete the blank forms found on the CD-ROM.)

(1):   *Your name* (not your signature).

   (1a): *The name of your trust.* Generally your name or your family name. For example, "The Smith Family Trust."

   (1b): *The signature of spouse.*

(2):   *Name of the county where you live.*

   (2a): *Name of the state in which you live.*

(3):   *State whether you are a widow or unmarried.*

(4):   *Name of your spouse if you are married or a widow.* If you are unmarried (never married or divorced) write "Not Applicable."

(5):   *Name(s) of your child(ren) and their birthdates.* If a child is an adult, you can simply list his or her name, a comma, and the words "an adult."

   Example: *"Bob Smith, born 12/25/02" or "Mary Lee, an adult."*

(6):   *Name(s) of the descendants now living of any predeceased children you have.*

   Example: *If your son, Bob, is now deceased, but left two children and one grandchild now living, you would list all three of those descendants of Bob and their relationship to you (i.e., grandchildren and great-grandchild).*

If you have no deceased child who left descendants now surviving, write "Not Applicable."

(7): *If you wrote "Not Applicable" for (6) above, insert "Not Applicable" here.*

If you have a predeceased child(ren) who left descendants now surviving and listed all of the descendants in (6) above, insert "no other."

(8): *List all bequests of personal, tangible property like furniture, cars, jewelry, etc.*

Example: *My green couch to my nephew, Bob Smith" for a will or "The Settlor's nephew, Bob Smith" or "Settlor's friends, Ned Jones and Mary Lee" for a trust.*

If you are not making any specific bequests of personal, tangible property, simply write "Not Applicable."

(9): *List who will receive your personal, tangible property that is not specifically disposed of in (8).*

Example: *"My nephew, Bob Smith" or "my friends, Ned Jones and Mary Lee" for a will or "The Settlor's nephew, Bob Smith" or "Settlor's friends, Ned Jones and Mary Lee" for a trust.*

If you want to leave your personal, tangible property to your residual beneficiaries listed in item (18), write "Not Applicable."

(10): *List any cash bequests to beneficiaries.*

Example: *"My nephew, Bob Smith, the cash sum of Ten Thousand Dollars ($10,000.00)" for a will or "The Settlor's nephew, Bob Smith, the cash sum of Ten Thousand Dollars ($10,000.00)" for a trust.*

If you do not wish to make any cash bequests, write "Not Applicable."

(11):   *List any specific bequests of real estate to beneficiaries.*

   Example: *"My nephew, Bob Smith, the residential real property located at 12 Maple Avenue, Los Angeles, CA."*

If you do not wish to make any specific bequests of real estate, write "Not Applicable."

(12):   *If you do not make any specific bequests of real estate in item (11), you can ignore item (12).* If you do make specific bequests of real estate in item (11), you need to do nothing at item (12) if you want the beneficiary of the real estate to receive the property free of all mortgages and liens. If, however, you want the bequest of real property to carry with it any mortgages or liens recorded against that property, you need to put a line through the sentence after item (12), and place your initials next to the end of the cross out BEFORE you sign your will or trust.

(13):   *Name of the life estate beneficiary.* If you are not giving a life estate to anyone, write "Not Applicable."

(14):   *Location of property subject to the life estate.*

(15):   *Name of person or entity that takes the life estate property after the death of the life estate beneficiary named in (13).*

(16)
and
(17):   *You are bequeathing the residue of your estate under your will or inter vivos trust; i.e., everything not already specifically bequeathed.* If you are leaving your residue in differing proportions, such as forty (40) shares to Bob and sixty (60) shares to Mary (or "All" to a single beneficiary), then you will leave the words between items (16) and (17) intact, cross out the words

"in equal shares" after item (16), and initial said cross-out BEFORE you sign your will or trust. (Remember to use shares, when possible, instead of percentages, to avoid problems when a beneficiary predeceases you.)

If, instead, you want to leave the residue of your estate to more than one beneficiary, in equal shares, you will cross out the words between item (16) and (17) and initial said cross out BEFORE you sign your will or trust.

If, instead, you want to leave all the residue to one person, cross out the words after (16) and (17) before you sign your will or trust.

If, in your will or trust, you are leaving everything to a trust under (19), then write "Not Applicable" at (18).

(18):   *Names of only the beneficiaries of the residue of your estate under your will or inter vivos trust* (if you crossed out the words between item (16) and (17)) or names of the beneficiaries of the residue of your estate and their proportions (if you crossed out the words "in equal shares" after item (17)).

> **Example:** *"To my nephew, Bob Smith, 20 shares and to my niece, Mary Lee, 80 shares" or "All to my nephew, Bob Smith" for a will or "The Settlor's nephew, Bob Smith, 20 shares and to the Settlor's niece, Mary Lee, 80 shares" or "All to the Settlor's nephew, Bob Smith" for a trust.*

If, in your will or trust, you are leaving everything to a trust under (19), then write "Not Applicable" at (18).

(19):   *The number of shares of the residue of your estate under your will or inter vivos trust going to the trust created under your will or inter vivos trust.* (If you are not leaving any portion of the residue of your estate to a trust created under your will, you should be using a different form.) If you are leaving everything to the trust created under your will, insert "All" after (19).

(20):   *Name of the beneficiary of the trust*—that is, the person who receives the income and/or principal of the trust.

(21):   *The age at which time the beneficiary receives one-half of his or her trust principal.* If you want the beneficiary to receive all of his or her trust principal at one age, write in "N/A" for "Not Applicable" and proceed to item (22).

(22):   *The age at which time the beneficiary receives the rest (or all) of his or her trust principal.* Typically, you will separate the ages at which time the beneficiary receives his or her trust principal. For example, one-half at age 25 and the remainder at age 30.

(23):   *Name of the beneficiary who receives the trust estate after the death of the life beneficiary of the trust.*

(24):   *Name of the beneficiary who receives the trust estate after the death of the life beneficiary, if the beneficiary in item (23) is then deceased.* If no such beneficiary is to be named in item (23), write "Not Applicable."

(25):   *Name of the person or entity who acts as the trustee.* You can nominate two trustees.

(26):   *Insert "co" before the word "trustee" and an "s" at the end of the word trustee if you nominate more than one trustee at item (25).* If you nominate one trustee at item (25), do nothing at item (26).

(27):   *Do nothing if you want the trustee you nominated to act without posting a surety bond.* Cross out the words "without bond" and initial said cross-out if you want your trustee to post a surety bond (recommended). (Remember that corporate trustees do not have to post bonds.)

(28):   *Name of the person or entity who is to act as the back-up trustee.*

(29):   *The age (anywhere from 18 years to 25 years) that the beneficiary will receive his or her custodial property.*

(30):   *Name of the person or entity who is to act as guardian or custodian.*

(31):   *Identify which codicil you are preparing. Is it the first codicil to your will or the second, third, or subsequent codicil?*

(32):   *Do nothing if you want the custodian(s) you nominated to act without posting a surety bond.* Cross out the words "without bond" and initial said cross-out if you want your custodian to post a surety bond (recommended). (Remember that corporate custodians do not have to post bonds.)

(33):   *Name of the person or entity who is to act as the back-up guardian or custodian.*

(34):   *Name of the person or entity who is to act as your executor.* (Remember that you can nominate two executors.)

(35):   *Insert "co" before the word "executor" and an "s" at the end of the word executor if you nominate more than one executor in item (34).* If you nominate one executor at item (34), do nothing at item (35).

(36):   *Do nothing if you want your executor to act without posting a surety bond.* Cross out the words "without bond" and initial said cross-out if you want your executor to post a surety bond (recommended). (Remember that corporate executors do not have to post bonds.)

(37):   *Name of the person or entity who is to act as the back-up executor.*

(38):   *Insert the date.*

(39):   *Insert the name of the city and state where your will or trust is being signed.*

(40):   *Sign your name.*

(41):   *First witness signs his or her name.*

    (41a): *Name of first witness.*

(42):   *First witness writes his or her address.*

(43):   *Second witness signs his or her name.*

    (43a): *Name of second witness.*

(44):   *Second witness writes his or her address.*

(45):   *Insert date of will you are amending.*

(46):   *Insert amendment words.*

    Example: *"I married Sue Smith on August 1, 2003."*

(47):   *You must select either Option 1 or Option 2.* If you select Option 1, then you must cross through the words between (47—Option 2 Start) and (47—Option 2B End) AND place your initials in the margin near the crossed through words.

    If you select Option 2, cross through the words between (47—Option 1 Start) and (47—Option 1 End) AND either cross through the words between (47—Option 2A End) and (47—Option 2B Start) OR cross through the words between (47—Option 2B Start) and (47—Option 2B End), depending on your selections. Place your initials on the margin next to the crossed-through words.

(48):   *Date that trust was executed (i.e., date trust was signed and notarized).*

(49):   *Name of original trustee or trustees.*

(50): *Insert "co" before the word "trustee" and an "s" at the end of the word "trustee" if there are two or more currently acting trustees at (49).*

(51): *Name of trustee in (49) if there is only one currently acting trustee. If there are two trustees in (49) then the word "either" should be inserted.*

(52): *Name of next successor trustee (after currently acting trustee).* If there are two or more trustees at (49), insert the name of the remaining acting trustee if he or she is to then act alone. Insert the name of the remaining trustee plus a successor trustee if the remaining trustee is to then act with another.

(53): *Attach a copy of all pages of the trust that relate to the powers of the trustee.* (In the forms located in this book, said trustee powers are always at Paragraph 4.6.)

(54): *Signature of currently acting trustee(s).*

(55): *Insert the street address and legal description (if possible) of all real property, account numbers of all brokerage and bank accounts, and any other property that you intend to transfer to the trust.*

(56): *Name of original trustee (see (4a)).* Very likely the settlor.

(57): *If the trust has been previously amended, cross out the following word "not."*

(58): *If the trust has been previously amended, cross out the following word "further."*

(59): *Cross out and initial the word "not" if you wish to include your adopted children as your descendants* (by law, your adopted children are already considered your children). In this sentence, you are addressing the question of whether your children's or grandchildren's adopted children are to be considered your issue (i.e., your descendants).

(60): *Cross out the words "codicil to his/her" if attaching affidavit to the will.* If attaching affidavit to a codicil, leave in.

Sample Forms

The accompanying CD-ROM contains 55 blank forms for various estate planning needs, including wills, inter vivos trusts, codicils, revocations, and appointments of guardians. The sample forms included in this appendix represent the most-used forms. They contain specialized information so that, should you need to include such information in your own documents, you can see how it can be worded.

LAST WILL AND TESTAMENT

I, (1)<u> ROBERT SMITH </u>, a resident of (2)<u> Los Angeles </u>
County, (2a)<u> CALIFORNIA </u>, being of sound and disposing mind and memory
and not acting under duress, menace, fraud or undue influence of any person
whomsoever, do make, publish and declare this to be my Last Will and Testament,
and I hereby expressly revoke all other wills, codicils, and testamentary writings
heretofore made by me.

FIRST. I declare that I am married. My spouse's name is
(4)<u> MARY SMITH </u>. I have the following children:
(5) THOMAS SMITH, born 5/31/03

I have a deceased child who left the following issue now surviving:
(6) NOT APPLICABLE

I have no other children and (7)<u> **NOT APPLICABLE** </u> deceased children who
left issue now surviving.

SECOND. I devise all of estate to my spouse. In the event my spouse should
predecease me then I leave all of my estate to my issue, by right of representation.

THIRD. I have intentionally and with full knowledge omitted to provide for my
issue, ancestors, relatives and heirs living at the time of my demise, except for such
provisions as are made specifically herein.

If any person who is or claims under or through a beneficiary of this Will,
or if any person who would be entitled to share in my estate if I died intestate,
should in any manner whatsoever, directly or indirectly, attack, contest or seek to
impair or invalidate in court any provision of the following:

A. This Will or any Codicil to this Will;

B. Any revocable or irrevocable Trust established by me;

C. Any beneficiary designation executed by me with respect to any insurance policy, any "Totten trust" account, any joint tenancy, any "transfer on death" account or any pension plan, or conspire or cooperate with anyone attempting to do any of the actions or things aforesaid, then I hereby specifically disinherit each such person and any devise, share or interest in my estate otherwise given to each such person under this Will or to which each such person might be entitled by law, is hereby revoked and shall pass and be distributed as though each such person had predeceased me leaving no issue or heirs whatsoever.

Any and every individual who asserts, or conspires or cooperates with any person who asserts, any claim against my Estate based on:

D. "Quantum meruit" theory;

E. Common law marriage, Marvin v. Marvin, 18 Cal. 3d 660 (1976) type of agreement or similar theory;

F. Constructive trust theory; or,

G. Oral agreement or written agreement which is to be proved by parole evidence, claiming that I agreed to gift or devise anything to such person or to pay such person or another for services rendered, regardless of whether a court may find that such agreement existed, then I hereby specifically disinherit each such person and any devise, share or interest in my estate otherwise given to each such person under this Will or to which each such person might be entitled by law, is hereby revoked and shall pass and be distributed as though each such person had predeceased me leaving no issue or heirs whatsoever.

FOURTH. I nominate and appoint my spouse as Executor hereunder without bond. In the event my spouse should decline, become unable or, for any reason, cease to serve as Executor then I nominate and appoint (37)＿＿＿ JOHN SMITH ＿＿＿＿＿ as Executor hereunder (36) without bond.

I authorize my Executor to sell (at either public or private sale), encumber, or lease any property belonging to my estate, either with or without public notice, subject to such confirmation as may be required by law, and to hold, manage and operate any such property.

FIFTH. All typed and handwritten "fill-ins" where directed above were made before the execution of this Will and are not initialed by me. All crossed through words and interlineations were made before the execution of this Will and are initialed by me.

Except as provided otherwise herein, the masculine, feminine, and neuter gender and the singular or plural number, shall each be deemed to include the others whenever the context so indicates.

IN WITNESS WHEREOF, I have hereunto set my hand this (38)_____3-1-07_____ at (39)____Upland_____, (2a)CALIFORNIA.

(40)____*Robert Smith*_____

The foregoing instrument, consisting of __4__ pages, including the page on which this attestation clause is completed and signed, was at the date hereof by (1)__ROBERT SMITH_____ signed as and declared to be his/her Will, in the presence of us who, at his/her request and in his/her presence, and in the presence of each other, have subscribed our names as witnesses thereto. Each of us observed the signing of this Will by (1)____ROBERT SMITH_____ and by each other subscribing witness and knows that each signature is the true signature of the person whose name was signed.

Each of us is now an adult and a competent witness and resides at the address set forth after his or her name.

We are acquainted with (1)_____ROBERT SMITH_____. At this time, he/she is over the age of eighteen years, and to the best of our knowledge, he/she is of sound mind and is not acting under duress, menace, fraud, misrepresentation, or undue influence.

We declare under penalty of perjury that the foregoing is true and correct.

Executed on (38)____3-1-07____ at (39)____Upland____, (2a)CALIFORNIA.

(41)____*C.U. Sign*____ Residing at (42)____123 Main St.____

____Upland California____

(43)____*M.E. Tue*____ Residing at (44)____345 Oak St.____

____Upland California____

LAST WILL AND TESTAMENT

I, (1)_____ ROBERT SMITH _____, a resident of (2)__ Los Angeles _____ County, (2a)____ California _____, being of sound and disposing mind and memory and not acting under duress, menace, fraud or undue influence of any person whomsoever, do make, publish and declare this to be my Last Will and Testament, and I hereby expressly revoke all other wills, codicils, and testamentary writings heretofore made by me.

FIRST. I declare that I am married. My spouse's name is (4)____ MARY SMITH _____. I have the following children:
(5) Thomas Smith, born 5/31/03

I have a deceased child who left the following issue now surviving:
(6) NOT APPLICABLE

I have no other children and (7)**NOT APPLICABLE** deceased children who left issue now surviving.

SECOND. I devise all of estate to my spouse. In the event my spouse should predecease me then I devise all my aforesaid estate to the Custodian under the Uniform Gift to Minors Act hereinafter named, to have and to hold upon the purposes and conditions of said act. I am secure in the knowledge that said Custodian will retain those items of personal use or sentimental value for my child or children in a manner I have made known or will make known to said Custodian.

My Executor, in making distribution to the Custodian, shall allocate the estate properties into as many shares as I have children then living and children then deceased who left issue then living. One such equal share shall be set aside for each of my children then living and one such equal share shall be set aside for the issue then living, by right of representation, of each of my children who are then deceased but left issue then living.

The Custodian may deposit any portion of a child's share in an I.R.C. 529 college savings plan for the benefit of said child.

Upon each minor attaining the age of (29)___25___ years, the Custodian shall deliver to said child all of the remainder of his or her share.

In the event a child should die before distribution to him or her of his or her share, his or her share on hand at the time of his or her death shall thereupon be apportioned and distributed to his or her surviving issue, by right of representation. If such child should die before complete distribution to him or her of his or her share and leave no surviving issue, then the balance of the share then on hand shall go and be distributed to my heirs to be determined according to the laws of the State of (2a)___California___ then in effect relating to the intestate succession of separate property not acquired from a predeceased spouse.

Each beneficiary hereunder is hereby prohibited from anticipating, encumbering, assigning, or in any other manner alienating his or her interest in either income or principal, and is without power so to do, nor shall such interest be subject to his or her liabilities or obligations, nor to attachment, execution, or other legal processes, bankruptcy proceedings or claims of creditors or others. The Trustee may, however, deposit in any bank designated in writing by a beneficiary, to his or her credit, income or principal payable to such beneficiary.

I nominate and appoint (30)___John Smith___ as Custodian hereunder (32) without bond. In the event he/she or both of them should decline to act, or for any other reason be unable to act as Custodian, then I appoint (33)___Betty Jones___ as Custodian hereunder (32) without bond.

THIRD. I have intentionally and with full knowledge omitted to provide for my issue, ancestors, relatives and heirs living at the time of my demise, except for such provisions as are made specifically herein.

If any person who is or claims under or through a beneficiary of this Will, or if any person who would be entitled to share in my estate if I died intestate, should in any manner whatsoever, directly or indirectly, attack, contest or seek to impair or invalidate in court any provision of the following:

A. This Will or any Codicil to this Will;

B. Any revocable or irrevocable Trust established by me;

C. Any beneficiary designation executed by me with respect to any insurance policy, any "Totten trust" account, any joint tenancy, any "transfer on death" account or any pension plan, or conspire or cooperate with anyone attempting to do any of the actions or things aforesaid, then I hereby specifically disinherit each such person and any devise, share or interest in my estate otherwise given to each such person under this Will or to which each such person might be entitled by law, is hereby revoked and shall pass and be distributed as though each such person had predeceased me leaving no issue or heirs whatsoever.

Any and every individual who asserts, or conspires or cooperates with any person who asserts, any claim against my Estate based on:

D. "Quantum meruit" theory;

E. Common law marriage, Marvin v. Marvin, 18 Cal. 3d 660 (1976) type of agreement or similar theory;

F. Constructive trust theory; or,

G. Oral agreement or written agreement which is to be proved by parole evidence, claiming that I agreed to gift or devise anything to such person or to pay such person or another for services rendered, regardless of whether a court may find that such agreement existed, then I hereby specifically disinherit each such person and any devise, share or interest in my estate otherwise given to each such person under this Will or to which each such person might be entitled by law, is hereby revoked and shall pass and be distributed as though each such person had predeceased me leaving no issue or heirs whatsoever.

FOURTH. I nominate and appoint my spouse as Executor hereunder without bond. In the event my spouse should decline, become unable, or for any reason, cease to serve as Executor, then I nominate and appoint (37)___John Smith___ as Executor hereunder (36) without bond.

I authorize my Executor to sell (at either public or private sale), encumber, or lease any property belonging to my estate, either with or without public notice, subject to such confirmation as may be required by law, and to hold, manage and operate any such property.

FIFTH. All typed and handwritten "fill-ins" where directed above were made before the execution of this Will and are not initialed by me. All crossed through words and interlineations were made before the execution of this Will and are initialed by me.

The masculine, feminine, and neuter gender and the singular or plural number, shall each be deemed to include the others whenever the context so indicates.

IN WITNESS WHEREOF, I have hereunto set my hand this (38)_____3-1-07_____ at (39)____Upland____, (2a)_California_.

(40)____*Robert Smith*____

The foregoing instrument, consisting of __5__ pages, including the page on which this attestation clause is completed and signed, was at the date hereof by (1)__Robert Smith__ signed as and declared to be his/her Will, in the presence of us who, at his/her request and in his/her presence, and in the presence of each other, have subscribed our names as witnesses thereto. Each of us observed the signing of this Will by (1)__Robert Smith__ and by each other subscribing witness and knows that each signature is the true signature of the person whose name was signed.

Each of us is now an adult and a competent witness and resides at the address set forth after his or her name.

We are acquainted with (1)__Robert Smith__. At this time, he/she is over the age of eighteen years, and to the best of our knowledge, he/she is of sound mind and is not acting under duress, menace, fraud, misrepresentation, or undue influence.

We declare under penalty of perjury that the foregoing is true and correct.

Executed on (38)__3-1-07__ at (39)__Upland__, (2a)__California__.

(41)__C.U. Sign__ Residing at (42)__123 Main St.__

__Upland California__

(43)__M.E. Tue__ Residing at (44)__345 Oak St.__

__Upland California__

LAST WILL AND TESTAMENT

I, (1)_____Mary Smith_____, a resident of (2)_____Upland_____ County, (2a)__California____, being of sound and disposing mind and memory and not acting under duress, menace, fraud or undue influence of any person whomsoever, do make, publish and declare this to be my Last Will and Testament, and I hereby expressly revoke all other wills, codicils, and testamentary writings heretofore made by me.

FIRST. I declare that I am married. My spouse's name is (4)_____Robert Smith_____. I have the following children:

(5)   Thomas Smith, born 5/31/07

I have a deceased child who left the following issue now surviving:

(6)   NOT APPLICABLE

I have no other children and (7) **NOT APPLICABLE** deceased children who left issue now surviving.

SECOND. I devise all of estate to my spouse. In the event my spouse should predecease me then I devise all my aforesaid estate to the Trustee hereinafter named, to have and to hold upon the uses, trusts, purposes and conditions here-inafter provided. I am secure in the knowledge that my Trustee will retain those items of personal use or sentimental value for my child or children in a manner I have made known or will make known to my Trustee.

My Executor, in making distribution to the Trustee, shall allocate the trust prop-erties into as many shares as I have children then living and children then deceased who left issue then living. One such equal share shall be set aside for each of my children then living and one such equal share shall be set aside for the issue then living, by right of representation, of each of my children who are then deceased but left issue then living. Said shares shall be held, administered, and distributed as provided in the following sections:

Each share set aside for a child of mine shall be held, administered and delivered for and to such beneficiary as follows:

1. The net income from the trust while said beneficiary is under 19 years of age and not a high school graduate shall be added to principal, from which the Trustee shall pay to or for the benefit of such beneficiary such sums as in the Trustee's discretion the Trustee shall deem necessary for such beneficiary's proper care, comfort, maintenance, support or education.

In making payments for the benefit of any beneficiary pursuant to this section 1, the Trustee shall construe his or her authority liberally to permit payments reasonably necessary to ease the financial burden on the guardian of the person of such beneficiary or other suitable individual with whom they reside, and on his or her family, resulting from such beneficiary's presence in his or her household.

2. Upon the beneficiary reaching 19 years of age or finishing high school (whichever occurs first), the Trustee shall pay to or apply for his or her benefit, from his or her trust, as much of the trust principal as the Trustee, in the Trustee's discretion, considers appropriate pursuant to sections 3 and 4 following.

3. After the beneficiary attains 19 years of age or finishes high school (whichever occurs first), the Trustee may, in the Trustee's discretion, pay to or apply from his or her trust, such amounts necessary for his or her education. For purposes hereof, education shall mean enrollment, attendance, and satisfactory progression towards a degree as a student at a recognized and accredited college, university, or similar institution of higher learning, including any graduate, professional school or college or trade school. Such educational payments and benefits shall include tuition, books, all direct educational costs and fees, and all

reasonable living and transportation expenses. Payments hereunder shall be made during vacation periods within the regular school term under which the beneficiary is attending school and during "summer vacation" or similar vacation period between the regular school terms.

The Trustee may invest any portion of a beneficiary's trust share in an I.R.C. 529 college savings plan for the benefit of said beneficiary.

4. If the beneficiary, his or her spouse, or any of his or her children should at any time or from time to time be in need, in the discretion of the Trustee, of funds due to illness, infirmity or other physical or mental disability or any emergency, the Trustee may relieve or contribute toward the relief of any such need or needs of the beneficiary by paying to him or her or using and applying for his or her benefit, such sum or sums out of the income and/or principal of his or her trust as the Trustee, in the Trustee's discretion, may deem necessary or advisable.

5. Upon the beneficiary attaining the age of 21 years, the Trustee shall begin to pay the beneficiary all of the net income, in monthly or other convenient installments, from the trust.

6. Upon the beneficiary attaining the age of (21) __25__ years, the Trustee shall distribute and deliver to such beneficiary one-half of his trust estate. Upon each beneficiary attaining the age of (22) __30__ years, the Trustee shall distribute and deliver to such beneficiary all of the remainder of his or her trust estate.

7. If, upon the attaining of the above ages, the Trustee suspects that said beneficiary may be abusing drugs, the Trustee may require the beneficiary to take a reasonable drug test. If the beneficiary fails said drug test, the Trustee shall defer said principal payment to the beneficiary until the beneficiary passes said drug test. After a failed drug test, subsequent drug tests shall be administered at six month intervals. In the event a beneficiary fails a drug test, the Trustee may use said beneficiary's trust estate to pay for a drug abuse rehabilitation program and may require the beneficiary to enroll and to complete said program as a condition precedent to the taking of a subsequent drug test.

8. In the event the beneficiary should die before complete distribution to him or her of his or her trust estate, his or her entire trust estate on hand at the time of his or her death shall thereupon be apportioned and distributed to his or her surviving issue, by right of representation. If such beneficiary should die before complete distribution to him or her of his or her trust estate and leave no surviving issue, then the balance of the trust estate then on hand shall go and be distributed to my heirs to be determined according to the laws of the State of (2a)___ California ___ then in effect relating to the intestate succession of separate property not acquired from a predeceased spouse.

9. Each beneficiary hereunder is hereby prohibited from anticipating, encumbering, assigning, or in any other manner alienating his or her interest in either income or principal, and is without power so to do, nor shall such interest be subject to his or her liabilities or obligations, nor to attachment, execution, or other legal processes, bankruptcy proceedings or claims of creditors or others. The Trustee may, however, deposit in any bank designated in writing by a beneficiary, to his or her credit, income or principal payable to such beneficiary.

10. If, at any time, a trust created hereunder shall, in the sole judgment of the Trustee, be of the aggregate principal value of Fifty Thousand Dollars ($50,000.00) or less, the Trustee may, but need not, terminate such trust and distribute the assets thereof in the Trustee's possession to the beneficiary or beneficiaries, at the time of the current income thereof, and if there is more than one beneficiary, in the proportion in which they are beneficiaries.

11. I nominate and appoint (25)__Betty Jones___ as (26)_____ Trustee hereunder (27) without bond. If he/she/both of them should die, resign, decline to act, or for any other reason, is unable to act as Trustee then I appoint (28)_____ John Smith _____ as Trustee hereunder (27) without bond.

THIRD. I have intentionally and with full knowledge omitted to provide for my issue, ancestors, relatives and heirs living at the time of my demise, except for such provisions as are made specifically herein.

If any person who is or claims under or through a beneficiary of this Will, or if any person who would be entitled to share in my estate if I died intestate, should in any manner whatsoever, directly or indirectly, attack, contest or seek to impair or invalidate in court any provision of the following:

A. This Will or any Codicil to this Will;

B. Any revocable or irrevocable Trust established by me;

C. Any beneficiary designation executed by me with respect to any insurance policy, any "Totten trust" account, any joint tenancy, any "transfer on death" account or any pension plan, or conspire or cooperate with anyone attempting to do any of the actions or things aforesaid, then I hereby specifically disinherit each such person and any devise, share or interest in my estate otherwise given to each such person under this Will or to which each such person might be entitled by law, is hereby revoked and shall pass and be distributed as though each such person had predeceased me leaving no issue or heirs whatsoever.

Any and every individual who asserts, or conspires or cooperates with any person who asserts, any claim against my Estate based on:

D. "Quantum meruit" theory;

E. Common law marriage, Marvin v. Marvin, 18 Cal. 3d 660 (1976) type of agreement or similar theory;

F. Constructive trust theory; or,

G. Oral agreement or written agreement which is to be proved by parole evidence, claiming that I agreed to gift or devise anything to such person or to pay such person or another for services rendered, regardless of whether a court may find that such agreement existed, then I hereby specifically disinherit each such person and any devise, share or interest in my estate otherwise given to each such person under this Will or to which each such person might be entitled by law, is hereby revoked and shall pass and be distributed as though each such person had predeceased me leaving no issue or heirs whatsoever.

FOURTH. I nominate and appoint my spouse as Executor hereunder without bond. In the event he/she should decline, become unable or, for any reason, cease to serve as Executor then I nominate and appoint (34)___Betty Jones___ as (35)_____ Executor hereunder (36) without bond.

I authorize my Executor to sell (at either public or private sale), encumber, or lease any property belonging to my estate, either with or without public notice, subject to such confirmation as may be required by law, and to hold, manage and operate any such property.

FIFTH: All typed and handwritten "fill-ins" where directed above were made before the execution of this Will and are not initialed by me. All crossed through words and interlineations were made before the execution of this Will and are initialed by me.

Except as provided otherwise herein, the masculine, feminine, and neuter gender and the singular or plural number, shall each be deemed to include the others whenever the context so indicates.

IN WITNESS WHEREOF, I have hereunto set my hand this

(38)_____3-1-07_____ at (39)_____Upland_____,(2a)___California___ .

(40)____Mary Smith____

The foregoing instrument, consisting of _7_ pages, including the page on which this attestation clause is completed and signed, was at the date hereof by (1)___Mary Smith___ signed as and declared to be his/her Will, in the presence of us who, at his/her request and in his/her presence, and in the presence of each other, have subscribed our names as witnesses thereto. Each of us observed the signing of this Will by (1)___Mary Smith___ and by each other subscribing witness and knows that each signature is the true signature of the person whose name was signed.

Each of us is now an adult and a competent witness and resides at the address set forth after his or her name.

We are acquainted with (1)___Mary Smith___. At this time, he/she is over the age of eighteen years, and to the best of our knowledge, he/she is of sound mind and is not acting under duress, menace, fraud, misrepresentation, or undue influence.

We declare under penalty of perjury that the foregoing is true and correct.

Executed on (38)___3-1-07___ at (39)___Upland___,
(2a)___California___.

(41)___C.U. Sign___ Residing at (42)___123 Main St.___

___Upland California___

(43)___M.E. Tue___ Residing at (44)___345 Oak St.___

___Upland California___

LAST WILL AND TESTAMENT

I, (1)___Richard Anderson_____, a resident of (2)___Cook_____
County, (2a)____ILLINOIS_____, being of sound and disposing mind and
memory and not acting under duress, menace, fraud or undue influence of any
person whomsoever, do make, publish and declare this to be my Last Will and
Testament, and I hereby expressly revoke all other wills, codicils, and testamentary writings heretofore made by me.

FIRST. I declare that I am married. My spouse's name is
(4)_____Sally Anderson_____. I have the following children:

(5) Mitchell Anderson, born 7-4-01

I have a deceased child who left the following issue now surviving:

(6) NOT APPLICABLE

I have no other children and (7)**NOT APPLICABLE** deceased children who
left issue now surviving.

SECOND. I devise the following personal, tangible property:

(8) My coin collection to my brother Ronald Anderson.

I devise to (9)_____Sally Anderson_____ all of my remaining
personal effects, household furniture and furnishings, trailers, boats, pictures,
works of art and art objects, collections, jewelry, silverware, wearing apparel,

148

collections, sporting goods, and all other articles of household or personal use or ornament at whatsoever time acquired by me and wheresoever situated.

I devise to the following persons the cash amount listed after their respective names:

(10) Michael Bower, $10,000
David Bower, $10,000
end of list

I devise to the following persons the real property described after their respective names. (12) Said real property is given free of all encumbrances or liens thereon.

(11) My sister Rhonda Anderson, a vacant lot located at
123 Main Street, Joliet, Illinois
end of list

I devise all of the rest, residue and remainder of my estate, real, personal and mixed, of whatsoever kind or character and wheresoever situated, of which I die possessed or to which I may in any manner be entitled, to the following persons or entities (16) in the proportions listed after their names (17) in equal shares.

(18) Sally Anderson, 100%
end of list

In the event any of the above named persons should predecease me or fail to survive me then his or her share shall lapse unless I have specifically named a person to take said bequest in the event of the first beneficiary's death.

Any beneficiary above who fails to survive me by thirty days shall be deemed to have predeceased me.

THIRD. I have intentionally and with full knowledge omitted to provide for my issue, ancestors, relatives and heirs living at the time of my demise, except for such provisions as are made specifically herein.

If any person who is or claims under or through a beneficiary of this Will, or if any person who would be entitled to share in my estate if I died intestate, should in any manner whatsoever, directly or indirectly, attack, contest or seek to impair or invalidate in court any provision of the following:

A. This Will or any Codicil to this Will;

B. Any revocable or irrevocable Trust established by me;

C. Any beneficiary designation executed by me with respect to any insurance policy, any "Totten trust" account, any joint tenancy, any "transfer on death" account or any pension plan, or conspire or cooperate with anyone attempting to do any of the actions or things aforesaid, then I hereby specifically disinherit each such person and any devise, share or interest in my estate otherwise given to each such person under this Will or to which each such person might be entitled by law, is hereby revoked and shall pass and be distributed as though each such person had predeceased me leaving no issue or heirs whatsoever.

Any and every individual who asserts, or conspires or cooperates with any person who asserts, any claim against my Estate based on:

D. "Quantum meruit" theory;

E. Common law marriage, Marvin v. Marvin, 18 Cal. 3d 660 (1976) type of agreement or similar theory;

F. Constructive trust theory; or,

G. Oral agreement or written agreement which is to be proved by parole evidence, claiming that I agreed to gift or devise anything to such person or to pay such person or another for services rendered, regardless of whether a court may find that such agreement existed, then I hereby specifically disinherit each such person and any devise, share or interest in my estate otherwise given to each such person under this Will or to which each such person might be entitled by law, is hereby revoked and shall pass and be distributed as though each such person had predeceased me leaving no issue or heirs whatsoever.

FOURTH. I nominate and appoint (34)_Sally Anderson_____ as (35)_____ Executor hereunder (36) without bond. In the event he/she or both of them should decline, become unable or, for any reason, cease to serve as Executor then I nominate and appoint (37)_Ronald Anderson____ as Executor hereunder (36) without bond.

I authorize my Executor to sell (at either public or private sale), encumber, or lease any property belonging to my estate, either with or without public notice, subject to such confirmation as may be required by law, and to hold, manage and operate any such property.

FIFTH. All typed and handwritten "fill-ins" where directed above were made before the execution of this Will and are not initialed by me. All crossed through words and interlineations were made before the execution of this Will and are initialed by me.

The masculine, feminine, and neuter gender and the singular or plural number, shall each be deemed to include the others whenever the context so indicates.

IN WITNESS WHEREOF, I have hereunto set my hand this (38)_____8-1-07_____ at (39)_____Chicago_____, (2a)__Illinois_____.

(40)__*Richard Anderson*_____

The foregoing instrument, consisting of <u>5</u> pages, including the page on which this attestation clause is completed and signed, was at the date hereof by (1) <u>Richard Anderson</u> signed as and declared to be his/her Will, in the presence of us who, at his/her request and in his/her presence, and in the presence of each other, have subscribed our names as witnesses thereto. Each of us observed the signing of this Will by (1) <u>Richard Anderson</u> and by each other subscribing witness and knows that each signature is the true signature of the person whose name was signed.

Each of us is now an adult and a competent witness and resides at the address set forth after his or her name.

We are acquainted with (1) <u>Richard Anderson</u>. At this time, he/she is over the age of eighteen years, and to the best of our knowledge, he/she is of sound mind and is not acting under duress, menace, fraud, misrepresentation, or undue influence.

We declare under penalty of perjury that the foregoing is true and correct.

Executed on (38)<u>8-1-07</u> at (39)<u>Chicago</u>, (2a)<u>Illinois</u>.

(41)<u>*C.U. Sign*</u> Residing at (42)<u>123 Main St.</u>

<u>Chicago, IL</u>

(43)<u>*M.E. Tue*</u> Residing at (44)<u>345 Oak St.</u>

<u>Chicago, IL</u>

LAST WILL AND TESTAMENT

I, (1)_____Chris Davis_____, a resident of (2)____Dade_____ County,
(2a)__Florida_____, being of sound and disposing mind and memory and not
acting under duress, menace, fraud or undue influence of any person whomsoever, do make, publish and declare this to be my Last Will and Testament, and I
hereby expressly revoke all other wills, codicils, and testamentary writings heretofore made by me.

FIRST.   I   declare   that   I   am   married.   My   spouse's   name   is
(4)_____Pat Davis_____. I have no children and no issue now
living of a deceased child.

SECOND. I devise all of my estate, real, personal and mixed, of whatsoever kind
or character and wheresoever situated, of which I die possessed or to which I may
in any manner be entitled, to my spouse.

If my spouse fails to survive me then I devise the following personal, tangible
property to the follow persons:

(8)   My complete vintage record collection to my brother
      Neil Davis

I devise to (9)_____Sid Davis_____ all of my remaining
personal effects, household furniture and furnishings, trailers, boats, pictures,
works of art and art objects, collections, jewelry, silverware, wearing apparel,
collections, sporting goods, and all other articles of household or personal use or
ornament at whatsoever time acquired by me and wheresoever situated.

I devise to the following persons the cash amount listed after their respective
names:

(10)   Veronica Davis, $10,000

I devise to the following persons the real property described after their respective names. (12) Said real property is given free of all encumbrances or liens thereon.

(11)   Not Applicable

I devise all of the rest, residue and remainder of my estate, real, personal and mixed, of whatsoever kind or character and wheresoever situated, of which I die possessed or to which I may in any manner be entitled, to ~~(16) in the proportions listed after their names~~ (17) in equal shares.

(18)   Sid Davis
        Mary Davis
        end of list

In the event any of the above named persons should predecease me or fail to survive me then his or her share shall lapse unless I have specifically named a person to take said bequest in the event of the first beneficiary's death.

Any beneficiary above who fails to survive me by thirty days shall be deemed to have predeceased me.

THIRD. I have intentionally and with full knowledge omitted to provide for my issue, ancestors, relatives and heirs living at the time of my demise, except for such provisions as are made specifically herein.

If any person who is or claims under or through a beneficiary of this Will, or if any person who would be entitled to share in my estate if I died intestate, should in any manner whatsoever, directly or indirectly, attack, contest or seek to impair or invalidate in court any provision of the following:

A. This Will or any Codicil to this Will;

B. Any revocable or irrevocable Trust established by me;

C. Any beneficiary designation executed by me with respect to any insurance policy, any "Totten trust" account, any joint tenancy, any "transfer on death" account or any pension plan, or conspire or cooperate with anyone attempting to do any of the actions or things aforesaid, then I hereby specifically disinherit each such person and any devise, share or interest in my estate otherwise given to each such person under this Will or to which each such person might be entitled by law, is hereby revoked and shall pass and be distributed as though each such person had predeceased me leaving no issue or heirs whatsoever.

Any and every individual who asserts, or conspires or cooperates with any person who asserts, any claim against my Estate based on:

D. "Quantum meruit" theory;

E. Common law marriage, Marvin v. Marvin, 18 Cal. 3d 660 (1976) type of agreement or similar theory;

F. Constructive trust theory; or,

G. Oral agreement or written agreement which is to be proved by parole evidence, claiming that I agreed to gift or devise anything to such person or to pay such person or another for services rendered, regardless of whether a court may find that such agreement existed, then I hereby specifically disinherit each such person and any devise, share or interest in my estate otherwise given to each such person under this Will or to which each such person might be entitled by law, is hereby revoked and shall pass and be distributed as though each such person had predeceased me leaving no issue or heirs whatsoever.

FOURTH. I nominate and appoint my spouse as Executor hereunder without bond. In the event my spouse should decline, become unable or, for any reason, cease to serve as Executor then I nominate and appoint (37)_____Neil Davis_____ as Executor hereunder (36) without bond.

I authorize my Executor to sell (at either public or private sale), encumber, or lease any property belonging to my estate, either with or without public notice, subject to such confirmation as may be required by law, and to hold, manage and operate any such property.

FIFTH. All typed and handwritten "fill-ins" where directed above were made before the execution of this Will and are not initialed by me. All crossed through words and interlineations were made before the execution of this Will and are initialed by me.

Except as provided otherwise herein, the masculine, feminine, and neuter gender and the singular or plural number, shall each be deemed to include the others whenever the context so indicates.

IN WITNESS WHEREOF, I have hereunto set my hand this (38)_____4-4-07_____ at (39)_____Miami_____, (2a)___Florida___.

(40)_____*Chris Davis*_____

The foregoing instrument, consisting of **5** pages, including the page on which this attestation clause is completed and signed, was at the date hereof by (1)__Chris Davis__ signed as and declared to be his/her Will, in the presence of us who, at his/her request and in his/her presence, and in the presence of each other, have subscribed our names as witnesses thereto. Each of us observed the signing of this Will by (1)____Chris Davis____ and by each other subscribing witness and knows that each signature is the true signature of the person whose name was signed.

Each of us is now an adult and a competent witness and resides at the address set forth after his or her name.

We are acquainted with (1)____Chris Davis____. At this time, he/she is over the age of eighteen years, and to the best of our knowledge, he/she is of sound mind and is not acting under duress, menace, fraud, misrepresentation, or undue influence.

We declare under penalty of perjury that the foregoing is true and correct.

Executed on (38)____4-4-07____ at (39)____Miami____, (2a)____Florida____.

(41)____*C.U. Sign*____ Residing at (42)____123 Main St.____

____Miami Florida____

(43)____*M.E. Tue*____ Residing at (44)____345 Oak St.____

____Miami Florida____

LAST WILL AND TESTAMENT

I, (1)_____Laura Tyler_____, a resident of (2)___Macon___ County, (2a)___Illinois___, being of sound and disposing mind and memory and not acting under duress, menace, fraud or undue influence of any person whomsoever, do make, publish and declare this to be my Last Will and Testament, and I hereby expressly revoke all other wills, codicils, and testamentary writings heretofore made by me.

FIRST. I declare that I am married. My spouse's name is (4)_____Elton Tyler_____. I have no children and no issue now living of a deceased child.

SECOND. I devise the following personal, tangible property to the follow persons:

(8)   My complete collection of depression area glass to Sebastian Wright

I devise to (9)_____Elton Tyler_____ all of my remaining personal effects, household furniture and furnishings, trailers, boats, pictures, works of art and art objects, collections, jewelry, silverware, wearing apparel, collections, sporting goods, and all other articles of household or personal use or ornament at whatsoever time acquired by me and wheresoever situated.

I devise to the following persons the cash amount listed after their respective names:

(10)   NOT APPLICABLE

I devise to the following persons the real property described after their respective names. (12) Said real property is given free of all encumbrances or liens thereon.

(11)   NOT APPLICABLE

I devise all of the rest, residue and remainder of my estate, real, personal and mixed, of whatsoever kind or character and wheresoever situated, of which I die possessed or to which I may in any manner be entitled, to (16) in the proportions listed after their names (17) in equal shares.

(18)   Elton Tyler should he survive me, then to Sebastian Wright

In the event any of the above named persons should predecease me or fail to survive me then his or her share shall lapse unless I have specifically named a person to take said bequest in the event of the first beneficiary's death.

Any beneficiary above who fails to survive me by thirty days shall be deemed to have predeceased me.

THIRD. I have intentionally and with full knowledge omitted to provide for my issue, ancestors, relatives and heirs living at the time of my demise, except for such provisions as are made specifically herein.

If any person who is or claims under or through a beneficiary of this Will, or if any person who would be entitled to share in my estate if I died intestate, should in any manner whatsoever, directly or indirectly, attack, contest or seek to impair or invalidate in court any provision of the following:

A. This Will or any Codicil to this Will;

B. Any revocable or irrevocable Trust established by me;

C. Any beneficiary designation executed by me with respect to any insurance policy, any "Totten trust" account, any joint tenancy, any "transfer on death" account or any pension plan, or conspire or cooperate with anyone attempting to do any of the actions or things aforesaid, then I hereby specifically disinherit each such person and any devise, share or interest in my estate otherwise given to each such person under this Will or to which each such person might be entitled by law, is hereby revoked and shall pass and be distributed as though each such person had predeceased me leaving no issue or heirs whatsoever.

Any and every individual who asserts, or conspires or cooperates with any person who asserts, any claim against my Estate based on:

D. "Quantum meruit" theory;

E. Common law marriage, Marvin v. Marvin, 18 Cal. 3d 660 (1976) type of agreement or similar theory;

F. Constructive trust theory; or,

G. Oral agreement or written agreement which is to be proved by parole evidence, claiming that I agreed to gift or devise anything to such person or to pay such person or another for services rendered, regardless of whether a court may find that such agreement existed, then I hereby specifically disinherit each such person and any devise, share or interest in my estate otherwise given to each such person under this Will or to which each such person might be entitled by law, is hereby revoked and shall pass and be distributed as though each such person had predeceased me leaving no issue or heirs whatsoever.

FOURTH. I nominate and appoint (34) <u>Elton Tyler and Sebastian Wright</u> as (35)___<u>co-</u> Executor hereunder (36) without bond. In the event he/she or both of them should decline, become unable or, for any reason, cease to serve as Executor then I nominate and appoint (37)_____<u>Rose Miller</u>_____ as Executor hereunder (36) without bond.

I authorize my Executor to sell (at either public or private sale), encumber, or lease any property belonging to my estate, either with or without public notice, subject to such confirmation as may be required by law, and to hold, manage and operate any such property.

FIFTH. All handwritten "fill-ins" where directed above were made before the execution of this Will and are not initialed by me. All interlineations were made before the execution of this Will and are initialed by me.

The masculine, feminine, and neuter gender and the singular or plural number, shall each be deemed to include the others whenever the context so indicates.

IN WITNESS WHEREOF, I have hereunto set my hand this (38)_____9-3-07_____ at (39)_____Decatur_____, (2a)___Illinois_____.

(40)___*Laura Tyler*_____

The foregoing instrument, consisting of _5_ pages, including the page on which this attestation clause is completed and signed, was at the date hereof by (1)__Laura Tyler____ signed as and declared to be his/her Will, in the presence of us who, at his/her request and in his/her presence, and in the presence of each other, have subscribed our names as witnesses thereto. Each of us observed the signing of this Will by (1)____Laura Tyler____ and by each other subscribing witness and knows that each signature is the true signature of the person whose name was signed.

Each of us is now an adult and a competent witness and resides at the address set forth after his or her name.

We are acquainted with (1)___Laura Tyler___. At this time, he/she is over the age of eighteen years, and to the best of our knowledge, he/she is of sound mind and is not acting under duress, menace, fraud, misrepresentation, or undue influence.

We declare under penalty of perjury that the foregoing is true and correct.

Executed on (38)_____9-3-07_____ at (39)___Decatur___, (2a)_____IL_____.

(41)___*C.U. Sign*___ Residing at (42)___123 Main St.___

___Decatur IL___

(43)___*M.E. Tue*___ Residing at (44)___345 Oak St.___

___Decatur IL___

LAST WILL AND TESTAMENT

I, (1)_____Joshua White_____, a resident of
(2)_____Polk_____ County, (2a)____Montana_____, being of
sound and disposing mind and memory and not acting under duress, menace,
fraud or undue influence of any person whomsoever, do make, publish and
declare this to be my Last Will and Testament, and I hereby expressly revoke all
other wills, codicils, and testamentary writings heretofore made by me.

FIRST. I declare that I am a
(3)_____Widower_____. My spouse's name was
(4)_____Margaret White_____. I have the following children:

(5) Jared White
     David White

I have a deceased child who left the following issue now surviving:

(6) Claire White

I have no other children and (7)__no other___ deceased children who left issue
now surviving.

~~SECOND. I devise the following personal, tangible property to the follow persons:~~

~~(8)~~

~~I devise to (9)_____ all of my remaining~~
~~personal effects, household furniture and furnishings, trailers, boats, pictures,~~
~~works of art and art objects, collections, jewelry, silverware, wearing apparel,~~

~~collections, sporting goods, and all other articles of household or personal use or ornament at whatsoever time acquired by me and wheresoever situated.~~

~~I devise to the following persons the cash amount listed after their respective names:~~

~~(10)~~

~~I devise to the following persons the real property described after their respective names. (12) Said real property is given free of all encumbrances or liens thereon.~~

~~(11)~~

I devise all of the rest, residue and remainder of my estate, real, personal and mixed, of whatsoever kind or character and wheresoever situated, of which I die possessed or to which I may in any manner be entitled, to (16) ~~in the proportions listed after their names~~ (17) or in equal shares.

   Jared White
(18) David White
   Claire White
   end of list

In the event any of the above named persons should predecease me or fail to survive me then his or her share shall lapse unless I have specifically named a person to take said bequest in the event of the first beneficiary's death.

Any beneficiary above who fails to survive me by thirty days shall be deemed to have predeceased me.

THIRD. I have intentionally and with full knowledge omitted to provide for my issue, ancestors, relatives and heirs living at the time of my demise, except for such provisions as are made specifically herein.

If any person who is or claims under or through a beneficiary of this Will, or if any person who would be entitled to share in my estate if I died intestate, should in any manner whatsoever, directly or indirectly, attack, contest or seek to impair or invalidate in court any provision of the following:

A. This Will or any Codicil to this Will;

B. Any revocable or irrevocable Trust established by me;

C. Any beneficiary designation executed by me with respect to any insurance policy, any "Totten trust" account, any joint tenancy, any "transfer on death" account or any pension plan, or conspire or cooperate with anyone attempting to do any of the actions or things aforesaid, then I hereby specifically disinherit each such person and any devise, share or interest in my estate otherwise given to each such person under this Will or to which each such person might be entitled by law, is hereby revoked and shall pass and be distributed as though each such person had predeceased me leaving no issue or heirs whatsoever.

Any and every individual who asserts, or conspires or cooperates with any person who asserts, any claim against my Estate based on:

D. "Quantum meruit" theory;

E. Common law marriage, Marvin v. Marvin, 18 Cal. 3d 660 (1976) type of agreement or similar theory;

F. Constructive trust theory; or,

G. Oral agreement or written agreement which is to be proved by parole evidence, claiming that I agreed to gift or devise anything to such person or to pay such person or another for services rendered, regardless of whether a court may find that such agreement existed, then I hereby specifically disinherit each such person and any devise, share or interest in my estate otherwise given to each such person under this Will or to which each such person might be entitled by law, is hereby revoked and shall pass and be distributed as though each such person had predeceased me leaving no issue or heirs whatsoever.

FOURTH. I nominate and appoint (34)_____Jared White_____ as (35)_____ Executor hereunder (36) without bond. In the event he/she/they should decline, become unable or, for any reason, cease to serve as Executor then I nominate and appoint (37)__David White_____ as Executor hereunder (36) without bond.

I authorize my Executor to sell (at either public or private sale), encumber or lease any property belonging to my estate, either with or without public notice, subject to such confirmation as may be required by law, and to hold, manage and operate any such property.

FIFTH. All handwritten "fill-ins" where directed above were made before the execution of this Will and are not initialed by me. All interlineations were made before the execution of this Will and are initialed by me.

The masculine, feminine, and neuter gender and the singular or plural number, shall each be deemed to include the others whenever the context so indicates.

IN WITNESS WHEREOF, I have hereunto set my hand this (38)__6-30-07_____ at (39)_____Polk City_____, (2a)__Montana_____.

(40)____*Joshua White*_____

The foregoing instrument, consisting of _5_ pages, including the page on which this attestation clause is completed and signed, was at the date hereof by

(1)___Joshua White___ signed as and declared to be his/her Will, in the presence of us who, at his/her request and in his/her presence, and in the presence of each other, have subscribed our names as witnesses thereto. Each of us observed the signing of this Will by (1)___Joshua White___ and by each other subscribing witness and knows that each signature is the true signature of the person whose name was signed.

Each of us is now an adult and a competent witness and resides at the address set forth after his or her name.

We are acquainted with (1)___Joshua White___. At this time, he/she is over the age of eighteen years, and to the best of our knowledge, he/she is of sound mind and is not acting under duress, menace, fraud, misrepresentation, or undue influence.

We declare under penalty of perjury that the foregoing is true and correct.

Executed on (38)___6-30-07___ at (39)___Polk City___, (2a)___Montana___.

(41)___C.U. Sign___ Residing at (42)___123 Main St.___

___Polk City Montana___

(43)___M.E. Tue___ Residing at (44)___345 Oak St.___

___Polk City Montana___

LAST WILL AND TESTAMENT

I, (1)_____Brian Black_____, a resident of (2)_____Alamo_____
County, (2a)___Texas_____, being of sound and disposing mind and
memory and not acting under duress, menace, fraud or undue influence of any
person whomsoever, do make, publish and declare this to be my Last Will and
Testament, and I hereby expressly revoke all other wills, codicils, and testamentary writings heretofore made by me.

FIRST. I declare that I am
(3)_____widowed_____. My spouse's name
was (4)_____Piper Black_____. I have the following children:

(5) Russell Black

I have a deceased child who left the following issue now surviving:

(6) NOT APPLICABLE

I have no other children and (7)__NOT APPLICABLE__ deceased children
who left issue now surviving.

SECOND. I devise all of estate to the Custodian under the Uniform Gift to
Minors Act hereinafter named, to have and to hold upon the purposes and conditions of said act. I am secure in the knowledge that said Custodian will retain
those items of personal use or sentimental value for my child or children in a
manner I have made known or will make known to said Custodian.

My Executor, in making distribution to the Custodian, shall allocate the estate
properties into as many shares as I have children then living and children then

deceased who left issue then living. One such equal share shall be set aside for each of my children then living, and one such equal share shall be set aside for the issue then living, by right of representation, of each of my children who are then deceased but left issue then living.

The Custodian may deposit any portion of a child's share in an I.R.C. 529 college savings plan for the benefit of said child.

Upon each child attaining the age of (29)___25___ years, the Custodian shall deliver to said minor all of the remainder of his or her share.

In the event a child should die before distribution to him or her of his or her share, his or her share on hand at the time of his or her death shall thereupon be apportioned and distributed to his or her surviving issue, by right of representation. If such child should die before complete distribution to him or her of his or her share and leave no surviving issue, then the balance of the share then on hand shall go and be distributed to my heirs to be determined according to the laws of the State of (2a)___Texas___ then in effect relating to the intestate succession of separate property not acquired from a predeceased spouse.

Each beneficiary hereunder is hereby prohibited from anticipating, encumbering, assigning, or in any other manner alienating his or her interest in either income or principal, and is without power so to do, nor shall such interest be subject to his or her liabilities or obligations, nor to attachment, execution, or other legal processes, bankruptcy proceedings or claims of creditors or others. The Trustee may, however, deposit in any bank designated in writing by a beneficiary, to his or her credit, income or principal payable to such beneficiary.

I nominate and appoint (30)___Todd Loring___ as Custodian hereunder (32) without bond. In the event he/she/they should decline to act, or for any other reason, is unable to act as Custodian then I appoint (33)___Michael Scott___ as Custodian hereunder without bond.

THIRD. I have intentionally and with full knowledge omitted to provide for my issue, ancestors, relatives and heirs living at the time of my demise, except for such provisions as are made specifically herein.

If any person who is or claims under or through a beneficiary of this Will, or if any person who would be entitled to share in my estate if I died intestate, should in any manner whatsoever, directly or indirectly, attack, contest or seek to impair or invalidate in court any provision of the following:

A. This Will or any Codicil to this Will;

B. Any revocable or irrevocable Trust established by me;

C. Any beneficiary designation executed by me with respect to any insurance policy, any "Totten trust" account, any joint tenancy, any "transfer on death" account or any pension plan, or conspire or cooperate with anyone attempting to do any of the actions or things aforesaid, then I hereby specifically disinherit each such person and any devise, share or interest in my estate otherwise given to each such person under this Will or to which each such person might be entitled by law, is hereby revoked and shall pass and be distributed as though each such person had predeceased me leaving no issue or heirs whatsoever.

Any and every individual who asserts, or conspires or cooperates with any person who asserts, any claim against my Estate based on:

D. "Quantum meruit" theory;

E. Common law marriage, Marvin v. Marvin, 18 Cal. 3d 660 (1976) type of agreement or similar theory;

F. Constructive trust theory; or,

G. Oral agreement or written agreement which is to be proved by parole evidence, claiming that I agreed to gift or devise anything to such person or to pay such person or another for services rendered, regardless of whether a court may find that such agreement existed, then I hereby specifically disinherit each such person and any devise, share or interest in my estate otherwise given to each such person under this Will or to which each such person might be entitled by law, is hereby revoked and shall pass and be distributed as though each such person had predeceased me leaving no issue or heirs whatsoever.

FOURTH. I nominate and appoint (34)_____Michael Scott_____ as (35)_____ Executor hereunder (36) without bond. In the event he/she/they should decline, become unable or, for any reason, cease to serve as Executor then I nominate and appoint (37)_____Todd Loring_____ as Executor hereunder (36) without bond.

I authorize my Executor to sell (at either public or private sale), encumber, or lease any property belonging to my estate, either with or without public notice, subject to such confirmation as may be required by law, and to hold, manage and operate any such property.

FIFTH. All typed and handwritten "fill-ins" where directed above were made before the execution of this Will and are not initialed by me. All crossed through words and interlineations were made before the execution of this Will and are initialed by me.

The masculine, feminine, and neuter gender and the singular or plural number, shall each be deemed to include the others whenever the context so indicates.

IN WITNESS WHEREOF, I have hereunto set my hand this (38)_____8-2-07_____ at (39)_____San Antonio_____, (2a)_____Texas_____.

(40)_____*Brian Black*_____

The foregoing instrument, consisting of **5** pages, including the page on which this attestation clause is completed and signed, was at the date hereof by (1)___**Brian Black**___ signed as and declared to be his/her Will, in the presence of us who, at his/her request and in his/her presence, and in the presence of each other, have subscribed our names as witnesses thereto. Each of us observed the signing of this Will by (1)___**Brian Black**___ and by each other subscribing witness and knows that each signature is the true signature of the person whose name was signed.

Each of us is now an adult and a competent witness and resides at the address set forth after his or her name.

We are acquainted with (1)___**Brian Black**___. At this time, he/she is over the age of eighteen years, and to the best of our knowledge, he/she is of sound mind and is not acting under duress, menace, fraud, misrepresentation, or undue influence.

We declare under penalty of perjury that the foregoing is true and correct.

Executed on (38)___8-2-07___ at (39)___San Antonio___, (2a)___Texas___.

(41)___*C.U. Sign*___ Residing at (42)___123 Main St.___

___San Antonio Texas___

(43)___*M.E. Tue*___ Residing at (44)___345 Oak St.___

___San Antonio Texas___

LAST WILL AND TESTAMENT

I, (1)_____Joshua Ross_____, a resident of (2)_____Clark_____
County, (2a)_____Washington____, being of sound and disposing mind and
memory and not acting under duress, menace, fraud or undue influence of any
person whomsoever, do make, publish and declare this to be my Last Will and
Testament, and I hereby expressly revoke all other wills, codicils, and testamentary writings heretofore made by me.

FIRST. I declare that I am (3)_____unmarried_____.
~~My spouse's name was (4)~~_____.-I have no children, living and no deceased children who left issue now living.

SECOND. I devise the following personal, tangible property:

(8) my baseball card collection to my nephew Thomas
     Ross

I devise to (9)_____my brother, Colin Ross_____ all of my remaining
personal effects, household furniture and furnishings, trailers, boats, pictures,
works of art and art objects, collections, jewelry, silverware, wearing apparel,
collections, sporting goods, and all other articles of household or personal use or
ornament at whatsoever time acquired by me and wheresoever situated.

I devise to the following persons the cash amount listed after their respective names:

(10) NONE

I devise to the following persons the real property described after their respective
names. (12) Said real property is given free of all encumbrances or liens thereon.

(11)

I devise all of the rest, residue and remainder of my estate, real, personal and mixed, of whatsoever kind or character and wheresoever situated, of which I die possessed or to which I may in any manner be entitled, to the following persons or entities (16) in the proportions listed after their names ~~(17) in equal shares.~~

(18)   my brother, Colin Ross, 100%
        end of list

In the event any of the above named persons should predecease me or fail to survive me then his or her share shall lapse unless I have specifically named a person to take said bequest in the event of the first beneficiary's death.

Any beneficiary above who fails to survive me by thirty days shall be deemed to have predeceased me.

THIRD. I have intentionally and with full knowledge omitted to provide for my issue, ancestors, relatives and heirs living at the time of my demise, except for such provisions as are made specifically herein.

If any person who is or claims under or through a beneficiary of this Will, or if any person who would be entitled to share in my estate if I died intestate, should in any manner whatsoever, directly or indirectly, attack, contest or seek to impair or invalidate in court any provision of the following:

A. This Will or any Codicil to this Will;

B. Any revocable or irrevocable Trust established by me;

C. Any beneficiary designation executed by me with respect to any insurance policy, any "Totten trust" account, any joint tenancy, any "transfer on death" account or any pension plan, or conspire or cooperate with anyone attempting to do any of the actions or things aforesaid, then I hereby specifically disinherit each such person and any devise, share or interest in my estate otherwise given to each such person under this Will or to which each such person might be entitled by law, is hereby revoked and shall pass and be distributed as though each such person had predeceased me leaving no issue or heirs whatsoever.

Any and every individual who asserts, or conspires or cooperates with any person who asserts, any claim against my Estate based on:

D. "Quantum meruit" theory;

E. Common law marriage, Marvin v. Marvin, 18 Cal. 3d 660 (1976) type of agreement or similar theory;

F. Constructive trust theory; or,

G. Oral agreement or written agreement which is to be proved by parole evidence, claiming that I agreed to gift or devise anything to such person or to pay such person or another for services rendered, regardless of whether a court may find that such agreement existed, then I hereby specifically disinherit each such person and any devise, share or interest in my estate otherwise given to each such person under this Will or to which each such person might be entitled by law, is hereby revoked and shall pass and be distributed as though each such person had predeceased me leaving no issue or heirs whatsoever.

FOURTH. I nominate and appoint (34)_____Catherine Ross_____ as (35)_____ Executor hereunder (36) without bond. In the event he/she/they should decline, become unable or, for any reason, cease to serve as Executor then I nominate and appoint (37)_____Colin Ross_____ as Executor hereunder (36) without bond.

I authorize my Executor to sell (at either public or private sale), encumber, or lease any property belonging to my estate, either with or without public notice, subject to such confirmation as may be required by law, and to hold, manage and operate any such property.

FIFTH. All typed and handwritten "fill-ins" where directed above were made before the execution of this Will and are not initialed by me. All crossed through words and interlineations were made before the execution of this Will and are initialed by me.

The masculine, feminine, and neuter gender and the singular or plural number, shall each be deemed to include the others whenever the context so indicates.

IN WITNESS WHEREOF, I have hereunto set my hand this (38)_____6-1-07_____ at (39)_____Vancouver_____, (2a)__Washington__.

(40)_____*Joshua Ross*_____

The foregoing instrument, consisting of __5__ pages, including the page on which this attestation clause is completed and signed, was at the date hereof by (1)__Joshua Ross__ signed as and declared to be his/her Will, in the presence of us who, at his/her request and in his/her presence, and in the presence of each other, have subscribed our names as witnesses thereto. Each of us observed the signing of this Will by (1)__Joshua Ross__ and by each other subscribing witness and knows that each signature is the true signature of the person whose name was signed.

Each of us is now an adult and a competent witness and resides at the address set forth after his or her name.

We are acquainted with (1)_____Joshua Ross_____. At this time, he/she is over the age of eighteen years, and to the best of our knowledge, he/she is of sound mind and is not acting under duress, menace, fraud, misrepresentation, or undue influence.

We declare under penalty of perjury that the foregoing is true and correct.

Executed on (38)_____6-1-07_____ at (39)_____Vancouver_____, (2a)____Washington_.

(41)____C.U. Sign____ Residing at (42)_____123 Main St._____

_____Vancouver Wa._____

(43)____M.E. Tue____ Residing at (44)____456 Oak St._____

_____Vancouver Washington_

LAST WILL AND TESTAMENT

I, (1)_____Joshua Ross_____, a resident of (2)____Clark____
County, (2a)____Washington____, being of sound and disposing mind and
memory and not acting under duress, menace, fraud or undue influence of any
person whomsoever, do make, publish and declare this to be my Last Will and
Testament, and I hereby expressly revoke all other wills, codicils, and testamentary writings heretofore made by me.

FIRST. I declare that I am
(3)_____Unmarried_____. ~~My spouse's name~~
~~was (4)~~_____. I have no children living and
no deceased children who left issue now living.

SECOND. I devise the following personal, tangible property:

(8) My baseball card collection to my nephew
      Thomas Ross

I devise to (9)_____Colin Ross_____ all of my remaining
personal effects, household furniture and furnishings, trailers, boats, pictures,
works of art and art objects, collections, jewelry, silverware, wearing apparel,
collections, sporting goods, and all other articles of household or personal use or
ornament at whatsoever time acquired by me and wheresoever situated.

I devise to the following persons the cash amount listed after their respective
names:

(10) NONE

I devise to the following persons the real property described after their respective names. (12) Said real property is given free of all encumbrances or liens thereon.

(11) My brother Colin Ross   123 Marine Dr. Vancouver Wa.

I devise to (13)_____my mother Catherine Ross_____ a life estate in the following property located at: (14)_____123 Marine Dr. Vancouver Wa._____. After the death of (13)_____Catherine Ross_____ said property shall go, outright, to (15)_____My brother Colin Ross_____ as the remainder person(s).

I devise all of the rest, residue and remainder of my estate, real, personal and mixed, of whatsoever kind or character and wheresoever situated, of which I die possessed or to which I may in any manner be entitled, to the following persons or entities (16) in the proportions listed after their names (17) in equal shares.

(18) My brother Colin Ross, 100%

In the event any of the above named persons should predecease me or fail to survive me then his or her share shall lapse unless I have specifically named a person to take said bequest in the event of the first beneficiary's death.

Any beneficiary above who fails to survive me by thirty days shall be deemed to have predeceased me.

THIRD. I have intentionally and with full knowledge omitted to provide for my issue, ancestors, relatives and heirs living at the time of my demise, except for such provisions as are made specifically herein.

If any person who is or claims under or through a beneficiary of this Will, or if any person who would be entitled to share in my estate if I died intestate, should in any manner whatsoever, directly or indirectly, attack, contest or seek to impair or invalidate in court any provision of the following:

A. This Will or any Codicil to this Will;

B. Any revocable or irrevocable Trust established by me;

C. Any beneficiary designation executed by me with respect to any insurance policy, any "Totten trust" account, any joint tenancy, any "transfer on death" account or any pension plan, or conspire or cooperate with anyone attempting to do any of the actions or things aforesaid, then I hereby specifically disinherit each such person and any devise, share or interest in my estate otherwise given to each such person under this Will or to which each such person might be entitled by law, is hereby revoked and shall pass and be distributed as though each such person had predeceased me leaving no issue or heirs whatsoever.

Any and every individual who asserts, or conspires or cooperates with any person who asserts, any claim against my Estate based on:

D. "Quantum meruit" theory;

E. Common law marriage, Marvin v. Marvin, 18 Cal. 3d 660 (1976) type of agreement or similar theory;

F. Constructive trust theory; or,

G. Oral agreement or written agreement which is to be proved by parole evidence, claiming that I agreed to gift or devise anything to such person or to pay such person or another for services rendered, regardless of whether a court may find that such agreement existed, then I hereby specifically disinherit each such person and any devise, share or interest in my estate otherwise given to each such person under this Will or to which each such person might be entitled by law, is hereby revoked and shall pass and be distributed as though each such person had predeceased me leaving no issue or heirs whatsoever.

FOURTH. I nominate and appoint (34)_____Catherine Ross_____ as (35)_____ Executor hereunder (36) without bond. In the event he/she/they should decline, become unable or, for any reason, cease to serve as Executor then I nominate and appoint (37)_____Colin Ross_____ as Executor hereunder (36) without bond.

I authorize my Executor to sell (at either public or private sale), encumber, or lease any property belonging to my estate, either with or without public notice, subject to such confirmation as may be required by law, and to hold, manage and operate any such property.

FIFTH. All typed and handwritten "fill-ins" where directed above were made before the execution of this Will and are not initialed by me. All crossed through words interlineations were made before the execution of this Will and are initialed by me.

The masculine, feminine, and neuter gender and the singular or plural number, shall each be deemed to include the others whenever the context so indicates.

IN WITNESS WHEREOF, I have hereunto set my hand this (38)_____6-1-07_____ at (39)_____Vancouver_____, (2a)_____WA_____.

(40)_____*Joshua Ross*_____

The foregoing instrument, consisting of __5__ pages, including the page on which this attestation clause is completed and signed, was at the date hereof by (1)___Joshua Ross___ signed as and declared to be his/her Will, in the presence of us who, at his/her request and in his/her presence, and in the presence of each other, have subscribed our names as witnesses thereto. Each of us observed the signing of this Will by (1)____Joshua Ross____ and by each other subscribing witness and knows that each signature is the true signature of the person whose name was signed.

Each of us is now an adult and a competent witness and resides at the address set forth after his or her name.

We are acquainted with (1)____Joshua Ross____. At this time, he/she is over the age of eighteen years, and to the best of our knowledge, he/she is of sound mind and is not acting under duress, menace, fraud, misrepresentation, or undue influence.

We declare under penalty of perjury that the foregoing is true and correct.

Executed on (38)_____6-1-07_____ at (39)____Vancouver____, (2a)__Washington__.

(41)____C.U. Sign____ Residing at (42)____123 Main St.____

____Vancouver Wa.____

(43)____M.E. Tue____ Residing at (44)____456 Oak St.____

____Vancouver Wa.____

SELF-PROVED WILL/CODICIL AFFIDAVIT

I, (1)_____Joshua Ross_____, the testator, sign my name to this instrument this ____1____ day of _____June_____, 20_07_, and being first duly sworn, do hereby declare to the undersigned authority that I sign and execute this instrument as my last will and that I sign it willingly (or willingly direct another to sign for me), that I execute it as my free and voluntary act for the purposes therein expressed, and that I am eighteen (18) years of age or older, of sound mind, and under no constraint or undue influence.

(1)_____Joshua Ross_____

Testator

We, (41)_____CU Sign_____, (43)_____ME Tue_____, the witnesses, sign our names to this instrument, being first duly sworn, and do hereby declare to the undersigned authority that the testator signs and executes this instrument as his last will and that he signs it willingly (or willingly directs another to sign for him), and that each of us, in the presence and hearing of the testator and in the presence of the other subscribing witness, hereby signs this will as witness to the testator's signing, and that to the best of our knowledge the testator is eighteen (18) years of age or older, of sound mind, and under no constraint or undue influence.

(41)_____*CU Sign*_____
(Witness)

(43)_____*ME Tue*_____
(Witness)

THE STATE OF ___Washington_____
COUNTY OF _____Clark_____

Subscribed, sworn to and acknowledged before me by (1)_____Joshua Ross_____, the testator and subscribed and sworn to before me by (41a)_____C.U. Sign_____, and (43a)_____M.E. Tue_____, witnesses, this ____1____ day of _____June_____, 20__07__.

_____*Noel Tara Public*_____ Notary

CODICIL TO LAST WILL AND TESTAMENT

I, (1)_____Robert Smith_____, a resident of (2)__Los Angeles__
County, (2a)__California_____, being of sound and disposing mind and
memory and not acting under duress, menace, fraud or undue influence of any
person whomsoever, do make, publish and declare this to be the (31)___First____
codicil to my Last Will and Testament dated (45)_____3-1-07_____

1. Paragraph _____First_____ is amended as follows:

(46) My daughter, Maria Smith, was born 1/7/08

2. All typed and handwritten "fill-ins" where directed above were made before the
execution of this Will and are not initialed by me. All crossed through words and
interlineations were made before the execution of this Will and are initialed by me.

3. I hereby ratify, confirm and republish my said Last Will and Testament, as
modified by this Codicil thereto.

IN   WITNESS   WHEREOF,   I   have   hereunto   set   my   hand   this
(38)_____3-20-08_____   at   (39)_____Upland_____,
(2a)____California_____.

(40)_____*Robert Smith*_____

The foregoing instrument, consisting of __2__ pages, including the page on
which this attestation clause is completed and signed, was at the date hereof by

(1)___Robert Smith___ signed as and declared to be his/her Codicil, in the presence of us who, at his/her request and in his/her presence, and in the presence of each other, have subscribed our names as witnesses thereto. Each of us observed the signing of this Codicil by (1)___Robert Smith___ and by each other subscribing witness and knows that each signature is the true signature of the person whose name was signed.

Each of us is now an adult and a competent witness and resides at the address set forth after his or her name.

We are acquainted with (1)___Robert Smith___. At this time, he/she is over the age of eighteen years, and to the best of our knowledge, he/she is of sound mind and is not acting under duress, menace, fraud, misrepresentation, or undue influence.

We declare under penalty of perjury that the foregoing is true and correct.

Executed on (38)___3-20-08___ at (39)___Upland___, (2a)___California___.

(41)___*C.U. Sign*___ Residing at (42)___123 Main St.___

___Upland Ca.___

(43)___*M.E. Tue*___ Residing at (44)___456 Oak St.___

___Upland CA___

INTER VIVOS TRUST

THE (1a)_____JOHNSON_____TRUST

The Settlor named below hereby declares as follows:

ARTICLE I
ESTABLISHMENT OF TRUST

Paragraph 1.01. Creation of Trust. This Trust Declaration has been entered into between (1)_____Nicholas Johnson_____ as Settlor and himself/herself as the Trustee. The Settlor, of (2) Benton County, (2a)_____Iowa_____, has transferred, or will transfer, to the Trustee of this Trust Declaration the property described in the attached Exhibit "A" which will constitute, together with any other property that may be added to this Trust Declaration, the Trust Estate of an express trust which shall be held, administered and distributed by the Trustee as provided in this Trust Declaration.

Paragraph 1.02. Trust Name. This Trust Declaration shall be known as the (1a)"_____JOHNSON_____TRUST" dated (48)_____8-28-07_____.

Paragraph 1.03. Definitions. As used in this Trust Declaration:

      A.   Settlor: The term "Settlor" shall refer to (1)_____Nicholas Johnson_____.

      B.   Trustee: The term "Trustee" or "Trustees" shall refer to whoever is serving as Trustee or Trustees under this Trust Declaration.

      C.   Trust Estate: The term "Trust Estate" shall refer to the property subject to this Trust Declaration.

ARTICLE II
OPERATION OF TRUST DURING THE LIFE OF SETTLOR

Paragraph 2.01. Net Income. During the life of Settlor the Trustee shall pay to or apply for the benefit of Settlor, in monthly or more frequent intervals, all of the net income of the Trust Estate.

Paragraph 2.02. Withdrawal of Principal. During the life of Settlor the Trustee shall also pay to or apply for the benefit of Settlor so much of the principal of the Trust Estate, up to the whole thereof, as Settlor shall direct.

Paragraph 2.03. Incapacity of Settlor. If, at any time during the life of the Settlor he or she shall become physically or mentally incapacitated so as to be unable to manage his or her affairs, whether or not a court of competent jurisdiction has declared him/her incompetent, mentally ill, or in need of a conservator, the Trustee shall pay to the Settlor or apply for the benefit of the Settlor such amounts of income or principal so that the Settlor enjoys a high standard of living commensurate with his/her estate and life expectancy. The interests of any other beneficiaries of this Trust are to be subordinated to the generous support of the Settlor. In this context "incapacitated" shall be determined by two physicians, at least one of whom is a geriatric specialist.

In regards to the amount of principal invasion by the Trustee for the Settlor, the Settlor is the primary beneficiary of this Trust Estate. The Settlor does not care if at his or her death the entire Trust Estate has been consumed by his or her needs. It is also the intent and desire of the Settlor that he/she live in his/her own home at all times, even if that requires the purchase of a new home to accommodate the in-home placement of twenty-four (24) hour nursing care.

The payments specified in this Section shall be made until the Settlor is again able to manage his or her own affairs, or until the death of the Settlor, whichever event may occur earlier.

Paragraph 2.04. Revocation of Trust. At any time during the life of the Settlor he or she may, by serving written notice on the Trustee, revoke the Trust created by this Trust Declaration, in whole or in part.

Paragraph 2.05. Amendment of Trust. At any time during the life of the Settlor, he or she may, by serving written notice on the Trustee, alter, modify or amend the Trust created by this Trust Declaration in any respect.

ARTICLE III
OPERATION OF TRUST AFTER DEATH OF SETTLOR

Paragraph 3.01. Collection of Assets and Payment of Debts: On the death of the Settlor the Trustee shall collect all assets belonging to the Trust Estate. As soon as practicable after the death of the Trustee, except as otherwise provided herein, shall pay from the Trust Estate the just debts of the Settlor (excluding any debts barred by provisions of law or not yet due), funeral expenses of the Settlor, and any inheritance, estate, or other death taxes that shall, by reason of the death of the Settlor, be attributable to the Trust Estate. This is not and shall not constitute a direction to pay all inheritance, estate or other death taxes from or charge the same to, the Trust Estate without apportionment.

Paragraph 3.02. Distribution of Trust Estate. Upon the death of the Settlor, and after payment of expenses as set forth in Paragraph 3.01, the Trustee shall hold, administer and distribute the Trust Estate as follows:

A. The Trustee shall distribute to the following persons the cash amount listed after their respective names:

(10)   NOT APPLICABLE

B. The Trustee shall distribute to the following persons the real property described after their respective names. (12) Said real property is given free of all encumbrances or liens thereon.

(11)   My wife, Lisa Johnson, 720 Maize Dr., Vinton, Iowa

C. The Trustee shall distribute to (13)__ NOT APPLICABLE a life estate in the following property located at: (14)_____. After the death of (13)_____ said property shall go, outright, to (15)_____ as the remainder person(s).

D. The Trustee shall distribute all of the rest, residue and remainder of the Trust Estate, real, personal and mixed, of whatsoever kind or character and wheresoever situated, to the following persons or entities (16) in the proportions listed after their names (17) in equal shares.

(18)   LISA JOHNSON, 100%
        end of list

E. Distribution of Trust Assets. With respect to the distribution of any trust estate upon termination of any trust, and partial distribution of any trust, the liquidation and distribution by the Trustee of the Trust Estate involved or the distributable portion shall commence immediately and be accomplished as rapidly as possible, and deliveries of the trust properties to the beneficiary or beneficiaries may be made in installments or series, retaining only reasonable reserves for final charges and expenses. In no event shall it be necessary for the Trustee to await an accounting to the Court, or any Court order, before releasing and distributing the majority of the Trust Estate to be distributed.

F. Undistributed Income. All the net income of the respective trusts or trust estates, not distributed, used or applied as otherwise provided herein, shall be accumulated and added to the principals of the respective trusts.

Upon the change or succession of any beneficiary, distribution of trust properties or any trust estate or any portion thereof, or upon setting aside, apportionment or division of any trust estate or upon the termination of a trust or any interest therein, the beneficial interest, properties or balance of trust estate at the applicable time and to be dealt with shall include any and all income accumulated, accrued, uncollected or held undistributed and all of such income shall likewise be distributed, set aside or apportioned to the next or succeeding beneficiaries, distributees, shares or trusts, retaining its character as income.

ARTICLE IV
TRUSTEES

Paragraph 4.01. Appointment of Trustees. (49)_____Nicholas Johnson_____ is appointed and confirmed as the Trustee(s). In the event (49)_____Nicholas Johnson_____ should die, refuse to act, or for any other reason be unable to act as Trustee then (25)_____Lisa Johnson_____ shall act as (26)____Trustee hereunder (27) without bond. In the event he/she/they should die, decline to act, or for any other reason, be unable to act as Trustee then (28)_____Michael Johnson_____ shall act as Trustee hereunder (27) without bond.

Paragraph 4.02. Substitute Trustee. The Settlor may appoint a substitute or successor Trustee to act as Trustee of any trust or trusts created hereunder in the place and stead of, or as successor to, any Trustee named in Section 4.01 above. Such substitution shall be in writing.

Paragraph 4.03. Trustee Liability. No person named as Trustee in this instrument or appointed as Trustee in the manner specified herein shall be liable to any beneficiary or to any heir of Settlor for the Trustee's acts or failure to act, except for willful misconduct or gross negligence. No such Trustee shall be liable or responsible for any act, omission or default of any other Trustee provided that they shall have had no knowledge of facts that might reasonably be expected to put the Trustee on notice of it.

Paragraph 4.04. Trustee Compensation. The Trustee shall be entitled to reasonable compensation for services rendered to the Trust or Trusts created hereunder.

Paragraph 4.05. Title to Trust Estate. The legal title to all property held in trust hereunder shall be, remain and become vested in the Trustee or successor Trustee from time to time acting hereunder, without any act of conveyance or transfer to or by or acceptance from, any succeeding, retiring or predecessor Trustee; however, any removed or resigning Trustee shall execute and deliver any and all conveyances and documents requested and reasonably necessary to transfer the trust estate and its assets to a successor Trustee. Each successor Trustee from time to time acting hereunder shall have all the rights, powers, immunities and authorities, discretionary or otherwise and the duties and obligations herein granted to the original Trustee. No successor Trustee shall be obligated to inquire into or be in any way responsible for the previous administration of any trust created herein or of the trust estate or for any act or default of any predecessor Trustee.

Paragraph 4.06. Powers of Trustee. To carry out the purposes of any trust created under this Trust Declaration, and subject to any limitations stated elsewhere in this Trust Declaration, the Trustee is vested with the following powers with respect to the Trust Estate, and any part of it, in addition to those powers now or hereafter conferred by law.

A. Power to Invest. To invest and reinvest the Trust Estate in every kind of property, real, personal or mixed, and every kind of investment, specifically including but not by way of limitation, corporate obligations of every kind, stocks, preferred or common, shares of investment trusts, investment companies, mutual funds, market index funds and mortgage participations which individuals of prudence, discretion and intelligence acquire for their own account, and any common trust fund administered by any Trustee under this Trust Declaration.

B. Power to Retain Property. To retain any property which was an asset of the Trust Estate during the Settlor's lifetime or received without consideration by the Trustee as long as the Trustee deems advisable whether or not of the character permitted by law for the investment of trust funds. The trust properties and investment need not be diversified and the Trustee shall have no duty to dispose or convert any trust assets to effect diversification.

C. Power to Manage Securities. With respect to securities held in this Trust Declaration, to have all the rights, powers and privileges of an owner, including but not by way of limitation, the power to vote, give proxies and pay assessments, to participate in voting trusts, pooling agreements, foreclosures, reorganizations, consolidations, mergers, liquidations, sales and leases and, incident to such participation, to deposit securities with and transfer title to any protective or other committee on such terms as the Trustee may deem advisable, to exercise and sell stock subscription or conversion rights and to hold securities in "street name."

D. Power of Sale, Exchange, Repair. To manage, control, foreclose, repossess, grant options on, grant easements on, sell (for cash), convey, exchange, partition, divide, improve and repair trust property.

The power to sell, at the termination of the trust, any trust property if the Trustee feels said disposition would assist in the distribution of the trust property at termination.

E. Power to Lease. To lease trust property for terms within or beyond the term of the trust and for any purpose, including exploration for and removal of gas, oil and other minerals; and to enter into community oil leases, pooling and unitization agreements, operating agreements or otherwise, and to create restrictions, easements or other servitudes thereon, to assign, partition, divide, subdivide, transfer to a corporation in exchange for stock, improve, repair, loan, reloan, invest and reinvest the trust estate or any part thereof.

F. Power to Insure. To carry, at the expense of the Trust Estate, insurance of such kinds and in such amounts as the Trustee shall deem advisable to protect the Trust Estate and the Trustee against any hazard.

G. Power to Commence or Defend Litigation. To commence or defend such litigation with respect to the Trust or any property of the Trust Estate as the Trustee may deem advisable, at the expense of the Trust Declaration.

H. Power to Compromise Claim. To compromise or otherwise adjust any claims or litigation against or in favor of the Trust Declaration.

I. Power to Employ Consultants. To employ any custodian, investment advisor, attorney, accountant or other agents to assist the Trustee in administration of this Trust Declaration and to rely upon the advice given by these agents. Reasonable compensation shall be paid to these agents for all services performed.

J. Power to Adjust for Tax Consequences. To take any action and to make any election the Trustee shall deem advisable to minimize the tax liabilities of this trust and its beneficiaries, to allocate the benefits among the various beneficiaries and to make adjustments in the rights of any beneficiaries or group of beneficiaries or between principal and income accounts, to compensate for the consequences of any tax election or any investment decision or administrative decision that has the effect of preferring one beneficiary or group of beneficiaries over others, provided such discretion shall not be exercised in any manner which will cause a loss of or a decrease in any marital or charitable deduction otherwise allowable in computing the Settlor's federal estate tax.

ARTICLE V
MISCELLANEOUS

Paragraph 5.01. No Assignment. Each beneficiary hereunder is hereby prohibited from anticipating, encumbering, assigning or in any other manner alienating his or her interest in either income or principal of any trust created under this Trust Declaration and is without power to do so nor shall such interest be subject to her or his liabilities or obligations nor to attachment, execution or other legal processes, bankruptcy proceedings or claims of creditors or others. The Trustee may require the personal receipt of a beneficiary as a condition precedent to payment, distribution or delivery of any amount, property or benefit hereunder. The Trustee may, however, deposit in any bank designated in writing, by a beneficiary, to her or his credit, income or principal payable to such beneficiary.

Paragraph 5.02. Principal and Income. Except as otherwise specifically provided in this Trust Declaration, the determination of all matters with respect to what shall constitute principal and income of each trust estate, gross income therefrom and net income distributable under the terms of the Trust Declaration, shall be governed by the provisions of the Revised Uniform Principal and Income Act as enacted in the State of (2a)_____IOWA_____, from time to time existing.

All taxes, assessments, fees, charges and other expenses incurred by the Trustee in the administration, protection and distribution of each trust, shall be a charge upon the trust estate and shall be paid out of the income and/or principal, in accordance with the aforesaid Act.

Paragraph 5.03. Savings Clause. Unless sooner terminated in accordance with other provisions of this Trust Declaration, any trust created hereunder shall terminate twenty-one (21) years after the death of the last surviving member of the group consisting of the Settlor and the issue of the Settlor who are living and in being at the date of death of the Settlor.

Paragraph 5.04. Payments to Minors and Incompetents. The Trustee, in the Trustee's discretion, may apply payments directly for the benefit of any beneficiary, rather than directly to such beneficiary and, in the case of a beneficiary who is a minor or who is under any other disability, make payment to the guardian, conservator of the person or estate of such beneficiary, custodian under the Uniform Transfers to Minors Act, parent or any other suitable adult with whom the beneficiary resides or by expending the same for the care, education, maintenance or other benefit of said beneficiary. In addition, the Trustee, in the Trustee's discretion, may make payments directly to a beneficiary who is a minor if, in the Trustee's judgment, the minor is of sufficient age and maturity to properly manage the money or property so paid. The Trustee shall not be required to see to the application of any such payment so made to any said persons, but his, her or their receipt therefor shall be a full discharge to the Trustee.

Paragraph 5.05. No Physical Segregation. There need be no physical segregation or division of the various trusts except as segregation or division may be required by the termination of any of the trusts or as specifically provided, but the Trustee shall keep separate accounts for the different undivided interests.

Paragraph 5.06. Distribution. In any case in which the Trustee is required, pursuant to the provisions of the Trust, to divide any parts or shares for the purposes of distribution or otherwise, except as the donee of any power of appointment affecting such property may have expressly provided otherwise in the instrument exercising such power, the Trustee is authorized, in the Trustee's absolute discretion, to make the division and distribution (pro rata or otherwise) in kind, including an undivided interest in any property or partly in kind and partly in money, and for this purpose, to make such sales of the trust property as the Trustee may deem necessary, on such terms and conditions as the Trustee shall see fit. Any asset which is encumbered shall be assigned subject thereto, and its value or amount shall be given effect less such indebtedness.

Paragraph 5.07. Non-Pro Rata Distributions. As to distribution or division of property in kind under and for the several trusts, excepting the initial establishment of any trust for a pecuniary amount, the Trustee shall be cognizant of the differences between the tax cost bases and current value and shall endeavor, insofar as is practicable to distribute or set aside to or for each beneficiary or distributee, assets or property carrying amount or portions of the total unrealized taxable gains or losses embodied in all the assets and properties involved commensurate with the share or portion of each beneficiary or distributee.

Paragraph 5.08. Distribution If All Beneficiaries Die Before Full Distribution. If at any time before full distribution of the Trust Estate, the Settlor is deceased and no disposition of the property is directed by this Trust Declaration, the Trust Estate or the portion of it not disposed of under the Trust Declaration, whichever the case may be, shall thereupon be distributed to the Settlor's heirs at law under the laws of intestate succession of the State of (2a)_____**IOWA**_____ then in effect for separate property not acquired from a predeceased spouse.

Paragraph 5.09. Additional Property. With consent of the Trustee, additional property may be added at any time from any source to any trust held under this Trust Declaration. No person dealing with the Trustee in any manner shall be under any obligation to see to the application of any money paid to the Trustee or to inquire into the validity, expediency or propriety of any act of the Trustee or into any of the provisions of any trust hereunder.

Paragraph 5.10. Fiduciary Capacity. All of the powers of the Trustee provided in this Trust Declaration shall be exercisable by the Trustee in the Trustee's fiduciary capacity and only in such capacity.

Paragraph 5.11. Corporate Office. No person shall, by reason of acting as Trustee, be in any way restricted or prohibited from holding office in any corporation in which any trust under this Trust Declaration holds securities or from receiving compensation from any such corporation for services performed as a director, officer or employee of such corporation or from purchasing, selling or otherwise dealing with the stock of any such corporation for the individual account of such Trustee or from voting the stock of any such corporation held by such trust, including voting those shares in favor of the Settlor or any other person.

Paragraph 5.12. Disclaimer of Powers. The Settlor may disclaim, release or restrict the scope of any power held in connection with any trust created under this Trust Declaration, including any administrative power, whether such power is expressly granted in this Trust Declaration or implied by law, by a written instrument specifying the power to be disclaimed, released or restricted and the nature of any such restriction. Any power disclaimed or released by the Settlor shall be extinguished except to the extent this Trust Declaration expressly provides that such power pass to another. This power shall be personal to the Settlor only and may not be exercised by any other person acting on behalf of the Settlor, including, but not limited to, any Trustee (other than the Settlor), Conservator, agent or guardian.

Paragraph 5.13. Notice. Unless the Trustee has received written notice of the occurrence of an event affecting the beneficial interest in any trust held under this Trust Declaration, the Trustee shall not be liable to any beneficiary of such trust for any distributions made or other actions taken by the Trustee in good faith as though such event had not occurred.

Paragraph 5.14. Invalidity of Any Provision. Should any provision of this Trust Declaration be or become invalid or unenforceable, the remaining provisions of this Trust Declaration shall be and continue to be fully effective.

Paragraph 5.15. Gender and Number. Except as provided otherwise herein, the masculine, feminine and neuter gender, and the singular or plural number, shall each be deemed to include the others whenever the context so indicates.

Paragraph 5.16. Law of Construction of Trust. This Trust Declaration, its validity, the construction of and all rights under the Trusts provided for in this Trust Declaration shall be governed by the laws of the State of (2a)_____IOWA_____.

Paragraph 5.17. No Contest. The Settlor has intentionally and with full knowledge omitted to provide for his/her issue, ancestors, relatives and heirs living at the time of his/her demise, except for such provisions as are made specifically herein.

If any person who is or claims under or through a beneficiary of this Trust, or if any person who would be entitled to share in the Settlor's estate if the Settlor died intestate, should in any manner whatsoever, directly or indirectly, attack, contest or seek to impair or invalidate in court any provision of the following:

    A. This Trust or any Amendment to this Trust;
    B. Any Will or Codicil to any Will executed by the Settlor;

C. Any beneficiary designation executed by the Settlor with respect to any insurance policy, any "Totten trust" account, any joint tenancy or tenancy by the entirety, any "transfer on death" account or any pension plan or conspire or cooperate with anyone attempting to do any of the actions or things aforesaid, then each such person and any devise, share or interest in the Trust or the Settlor's Estate otherwise given to each such person under this Trust or the Settlor's Estate to which each such person might be entitled by law, is hereby revoked and shall pass and be distributed as though each such person had predeceased the Settlor leaving no issue or heirs whatsoever.

Any and every individual who asserts, or conspires or cooperates with any person who asserts, any claim against this Trust or the Estate of the Settlor of this Trust based on:

D. "Quantum meruit" theory;

E. Common law marriage, Marvin v. Marvin, 18 Cal. 3d 660 (1976) type of agreement or similar theory;

F. Constructive trust theory; or,

G. Oral agreement or written agreement which is to be proved by parole evidence, claiming that Settlor agreed to gift or devise anything to such person or to pay such person or another for services rendered, regardless of whether a court may find that such agreement existed, then each such person is disinherited and any devise, share or interest in this Trust or the Settlor's Estate otherwise given to each such person under this Trust or the Settlor's Estate or to which each such person might be entitled by law, is hereby revoked and shall pass and be distributed as though each such person had predeceased the Settlor leaving no issue or heirs whatsoever.

The Trustee is specifically authorized to defend any such attack, contest, claim or other proceeding of any nature concerning this Trust or of any provision hereof, and to employ legal counsel therefor, all at the expense of the Trust.

Paragraph 5.18. Survival. If any person fails to survive the Settlor by thirty (30) days, for all purposes of this Trust Declaration the person shall be considered to have predeceased the Settlor.

Paragraph 5.19. All typed and handwritten "fill-ins" where directed above were made before the execution of this Declaration of Trust and are not initialed by the Settlor. All crossed through words and interlineations were made before the execution of this Trust and are initialed by the Settlor.

CERTIFICATION OF SETTLOR

I certify that:

A.   I have read the foregoing Trust Declaration;

B.   The foregoing Trust Declaration correctly states the terms and conditions under which the Trust Estate is to be held, managed, administered and disposed of by the Trustee;

C.   As the Settlor named in such Trust Declaration, I approve such Trust Declaration in all particulars; and,

D.   As the Trustee named in such Trust Declaration, I approve and accept the Trust provided for in such Declaration.

Dated: 8-28-07   (40)___*Nicholas Johnson*_____

                         (1)_NICHOLAS JOHNSON_, Settlor

                         (54)___*Nicholas Johnson*_____

                         (49)_NICHOLAS JOHNSON_, Trustee

STATE OF   (2a)_____IOWA_____)
) ss.
COUNTY OF (2)_____BENTON_____)

On ___August 28___, 20_07_ before me, the undersigned, a Notary Public in and for said county and state, personally appeared (1)___NICHOLAS JOHNSON___, personally known to me (or proved to me on the basis of satisfactory evidence) to be the person(s) whose name(s) is/are subscribed to the within instrument and acknowledged that he/she/they executed the same in his/her/their authorized capacity(ies), and that by his/her/their signature(s) on the instrument the person(s), or the entity upon behalf of which the person(s) acted, executed the instrument.

WITNESS my hand and official seal.

_____*Noel Tara Public*_____
Notary Public in and for said County and State

EXHIBIT A

Property Declared to be assets of the (1a)_____ JOHNSON_____
TRUST dated (48)___8-28-07_____ :

(55)

1. 720 Maize Dr. Vinton Iowa
2. 1st Famers' Bank Account Number 123-456-7890
3. 800 shares, common, IBM
4. All personal property

INTER VIVOS TRUST

THE (1a)_____**BROWN**_____ TRUST

The Settlor named below hereby declares as follows:

ARTICLE I
ESTABLISHMENT OF TRUST

Paragraph 1.01. Creation of Trust. This Trust Declaration has been entered into between (1)_____**STEPHEN BROWN**_____ as Settlor and himself/herself as the Trustee. The Settlor, of (2)_____**Barnstable**_____ County, (2a)__**Massachusetts**___, has transferred, or will transfer, to the Trustee of this Trust Declaration the property described in the attached Exhibit "A" which will constitute, together with any other property that may be added to this Trust Declaration, the Trust Estate of an express trust which shall be held, administered and distributed by the Trustee as provided in this Trust Declaration.

Paragraph 1.02. Trust Name. This Trust Declaration shall be known as the (1a)"_____**BROWN**_____TRUST" dated (48)_____**11-1-07**_____.

Paragraph 1.03. Definitions. As used in this Trust Declaration:

A. Settlor: The term "Settlor" shall refer to (1)__**STEPHEN BROWN**__.

B. Trustee: The term "Trustee" or "Trustees" shall refer to whoever is serving as Trustee or Trustees under this Trust Declaration.

C. Trust Estate: The term "Trust Estate" shall refer to the property subject to this Trust Declaration.

D. Issue: The term "issue" shall refer only to a person who is a lineal descendant of any degree of the Settlor and shall (59) ~~not~~ include adopted persons.

ARTICLE II
OPERATION OF TRUST DURING THE LIFE OF SETTLOR

Paragraph 2.01. Net Income. During the life of Settlor the Trustee shall pay to or apply for the benefit of Settlor, in monthly or more frequent intervals, all of the net income of the Trust Estate.

Paragraph 2.02. Withdrawal of Principal. During the life of Settlor the Trustee shall also pay to or apply for the benefit of Settlor so much of the principal of the Trust Estate, up to the whole thereof, as Settlor shall direct.

Paragraph 2.03. Incapacity of Settlor. If, at any time during the life of the Settlor he/she shall become physically or mentally incapacitated so as to be unable to manage his or her affairs, whether or not a court of competent jurisdiction has declared him or her incompetent, mentally ill, or in need of a conservator, the Trustee shall pay to the Settlor or apply for the benefit of the Settlor such amounts of income or principal so that the Settlor enjoys a high standard of living commensurate with his/her estate or life expectancy. The interests of any other beneficiaries of this Trust are to be subordinated to the generous support of the Settlor. In this context "incapacitated" shall be determined by two physicians, at least one of whom is a geriatric specialists.

In regards to the amount of principal invasion by the Trustee for the Settlor, the Settlor is the primary beneficiary of this Trust Estate. The Settlor does not care if at his or her death the entire Trust Estate has been consumed by his or her needs. It is also the intent and desire of the Settlor that he/she live in his/her own home at all times, even if that requires the purchase of a new home to accommodate the in-home placement of twenty-four (24) hour nursing care.

The payments specified in this Section shall be made until the Settlor is again able to manage his or her own affairs, or until the death of the Settlor, whichever event may occur earlier.

Paragraph 2.04. Revocation of Trust. At any time during the life of the Settlor he/she may, by serving written notice on the Trustee, revoke the Trust created by this Trust Declaration, in whole or in part.

Paragraph 2.05. Amendment of Trust. At any time during the life of the Settlor, he/she may, by serving written notice on the Trustee, alter, modify or amend the Trust created by this Trust Declaration in any respect.

ARTICLE III
OPERATION OF TRUST AFTER DEATH OF SETTLOR

Paragraph 3.01. Collection of Assets and Payment of Debts: On the death of the Settlor the Trustee shall collect all assets belonging to the Trust Estate. As soon as practicable after the death of the Trustee, except as otherwise provided herein, shall pay from the Trust Estate the just debts of the Settlor (excluding any debts barred by provisions of law or not yet due), funeral expenses of the Settlor, and any inheritance, estate, or other death taxes that shall, by reason of the death of the Settlor, be attributable to the Trust Estate. This is not and shall not constitute a direction to pay all inheritance, estate or other death taxes from or charge the same to, the Trust Estate without apportionment.

Paragraph 3.02. Distribution of Trust Estate. Upon the death of the Settlor, and after payment of expenses as set forth in Paragraph 3.01, the Trustee shall hold, administer and distribute the Trust Estate as follows:

A. The Trustee shall distribute to the following persons the cash amount listed after their respective names:

(10) NOT APPLICABLE

B. The Trustee shall distribute to the following persons the real property described after their respective names. (12) Said real property is given free of all encumbrances or liens thereon.
(11)

C. The Trustee shall distribute to (13)__Elizabeth Brown__ a life estate in the following property located at: (14)__4359 Red Roof Road__ - __Barnstable, MA__. After the death of (13)__Elizabeth Brown__ said property shall go, outright, to (15)__Anthony Brown__ as the remainder person as described in Paragraph D.

D. The Trustee shall distribute all of the rest, residue and remainder of the Trust Estate, real, personal and mixed, of whatsoever kind or character and wheresoever situated, to the following persons or entities (16) in the proportions listed after their names (17) in equal shares.
(18)   **NONE**

and (19)__ALL__ shares to the Trustee hereinafter named, to have and to hold for the benefit of (20)__Anthony Brown__ upon the uses, trusts, purposes and conditions hereinafter provided.

The Trustee, shall allocate the trust properties into as many shares as there are children of the Settlor then living and children of the Settlor then deceased who left issue then living. One such equal share shall be set aside for each of the

Settlor's children then living and one such equal share shall be set aside for the issue then living, by right of representation, of each of the Settlor's children who are then deceased but left issue then living. Said shares shall be held, administered, and distributed as provided in the following sections:

Each share set aside for a child of the Settlor shall be held, administered and delivered for and to such beneficiary as follows:

1. The net income from the trust while said beneficiary is under 19 years of age and not a high school graduate shall be added to principal, from which the Trustee shall pay to or for the benefit of such beneficiary such sums as in the Trustee's discretion the Trustee shall deem necessary for such beneficiary's proper care, comfort, maintenance, support or education.

In making payments for the benefit of any beneficiary pursuant to this section 1, the Trustee shall construe his or her authority liberally to permit payments reasonably necessary to ease the financial burden on the guardian of the person of such beneficiary or other suitable individual with whom they reside, and on his or her family, resulting from such beneficiary's presence in his or her household.

2. Upon the beneficiary reaching 19 years of age or finishing high school (whichever occurs first), the Trustee shall pay to or apply for his or her benefit, from his or her trust, as much of the trust principal as the Trustee, in the Trustee's discretion, considers appropriate pursuant to sections 3 and 4 following.

3. After the beneficiary attains 19 years of age or finishes high school (whichever occurs first), the Trustee may, in the Trustee's discretion, pay to or apply from his or her trust, such amounts necessary for his or her education. For purposes hereof, education shall mean enrollment, attendance, and satisfactory progression towards a degree as a student at a recognized and accredited college, university, or similar institution of higher learning, including any graduate, professional school or college or trade school. Such educational payments and benefits shall include tuition, books, all direct educational costs and fees, and all reasonable living and transportation expenses. Payments hereunder shall be made during vacation periods within the regular school term

under which the beneficiary is attending school and during "summer vacation" or similar vacation period between the regular school terms.

The Trustee may invest any portion of a beneficiary's trust share in an I.R.C. 529 college savings plan for the benefit of said beneficiary.

4. If the beneficiary, his or her spouse, or any of his or her children should at any time or from time to time be in need, in the discretion of the Trustee, of funds due to illness, infirmity or other physical or mental disability or any emergency, the Trustee may relieve or contribute toward the relief of any such need or needs of the beneficiary by paying to him or her or using and applying for his or her benefit, such sum or sums out of the income and/or principal of his or her trust as the Trustee, in the Trustee's discretion, may deem necessary or advisable.

5. Upon the beneficiary attaining the age of 21 years, the Trustee shall begin to pay the beneficiary all of the net income, in monthly or other convenient installments, from the trust.

6. Upon the beneficiary attaining the age of (21)__25__ years, the Trustee shall distribute and deliver to such beneficiary one-half of his or her trust estate. Upon each beneficiary attaining the age of (22)__30__ years, the Trustee shall distribute and deliver to such beneficiary all of the remainder of his or her trust estate.

7. If, upon the beneficiary attaining the above ages, the Trustee suspects that said beneficiary may be abusing drugs, the Trustee may require the beneficiary to take a reasonable drug test. If the beneficiary fails said drug test, the Trustee shall defer said principal payment to the beneficiary until the beneficiary passes said drug test. After a failed drug test, subsequent drug tests shall be administered at six month intervals. In the event a beneficiary fails a drug test, the Trustee may use said beneficiary's trust estate to pay for a drug abuse rehabilitation program and may require the beneficiary to enroll and to complete said program as a condition precedent to the taking of a subsequent drug test.

8. In the event the beneficiary should die before complete distribution to him or her of his or her trust estate, his or her entire trust estate on hand at the time of his or her death shall thereupon be apportioned and distributed to his or her surviving issue, by right of representation. If such beneficiary should die before complete distribution to him or her of his or her trust estate and leave no surviving issue, then the balance of the trust estate then on hand

shall go and be distributed to the Settlor's heirs to be determined according to the laws of the State of (2a) __Massachusetts__ then in effect relating to the intestate succession of separate property not acquired from a predeceased spouse.

9. If, at any time, a trust created hereunder shall, in the sole judgment of the Trustee, be of the aggregate principal value of Fifty Thousand Dollars ($50,000.00) or less, the Trustee may, but need not, terminate such trust and distribute the assets thereof in the Trustee's possession to the beneficiary or beneficiaries, at the time of the current income thereof, and if there is more than one beneficiary, in the proportion in which they are beneficiaries.

E. Distribution of Trust Assets. With respect to the distribution of any trust estate upon termination of any trust, and partial distribution of any trust, the liquidation and distribution by the Trustee of the Trust Estate involved or the distributable portion shall commence immediately and be accomplished as rapidly as possible, and deliveries of the trust properties to the beneficiary or beneficiaries may be made in installments or series, retaining only reasonable reserves for final charges and expenses. In no event shall it be necessary for the Trustee to await an accounting to the Court, or any Court order, before releasing and distributing the majority of the Trust Estate to be distributed.

F. Undistributed Income. All the net income of the respective trusts or trust estates, not distributed, used or applied as otherwise provided herein, shall be accumulated and added to the principals of the respective trusts.

Upon the change or succession of any beneficiary, distribution of trust properties or any trust estate or any portion thereof, or upon setting aside, apportionment or division of any trust estate or upon the termination of a trust or any interest therein, the beneficial interest, properties or balance of trust estate at the applicable time and to be dealt with shall include any and all income accumulated, accrued, uncollected or held undistributed and all of such income shall likewise be distributed, set aside or apportioned to the next or succeeding beneficiaries, distributees, shares or trusts, retaining its character as income.

ARTICLE IV

TRUSTEES

Paragraph 4.01. Appointment of Trustees. (49)___**STEPHEN BROWN**___ is appointed and confirmed as the Trustee(s). In the event (49)_**STEPHEN BROWN**___ should die, refuse to act, or for any other reason be unable to act as Trustee then (25)_**ELIZABETH BROWN**_ shall act as (26)____Trustee hereunder (27) without bond. In the event he/she/they should die, decline to act, or for any other reason, be unable to act as Trustee then (28)___**BRIAN BROWN**___ shall act as Trustee hereunder (27) without bond.

Paragraph 4.02. Substitute Trustee. The Settlor may appoint a substitute or successor Trustee to act as Trustee of any trust or trusts created hereunder in the place and stead of, or as successor to, any Trustee named in Section 4.01 above. Such substitution shall be in writing.

Paragraph 4.03. Trustee Liability. No person named as Trustee in this instrument or appointed as Trustee in the manner specified herein shall be liable to any beneficiary or to any heir of Settlor for the Trustee's acts or failure to act, except for willful misconduct or gross negligence. No such Trustee shall be liable or responsible for any act, omission or default of any other Trustee provided that they shall have had no knowledge of facts that might reasonably be expected to put the Trustee on notice of it.

Paragraph 4.04. Trustee Compensation. The Trustee shall be entitled to reasonable compensation for services rendered to the Trust or Trusts created hereunder.

Paragraph 4.05. Title to Trust Estate. The legal title to all property held in trust hereunder shall be, remain and become vested in the Trustee or successor Trustee from time to time acting hereunder, without any act of conveyance or transfer to or by or acceptance from, any succeeding, retiring or predecessor Trustee;

however, any removed or resigning Trustee shall execute and deliver any and all conveyances and documents requested and reasonably necessary to transfer the trust estate and its assets to a successor Trustee. Each successor Trustee from time to time acting hereunder shall have all the rights, powers, immunities and authorities, discretionary or otherwise and the duties and obligations herein granted to the original Trustee. No successor Trustee shall be obligated to inquire into or be in any way responsible for the previous administration of any trust created herein or of the trust estate or for any act or default of any predecessor Trustee.

Paragraph 4.06. Powers of Trustee. To carry out the purposes of any trust created under this Trust Declaration, and subject to any limitations stated elsewhere in this Trust Declaration, the Trustee is vested with the following powers with respect to the Trust Estate, and any part of it, in addition to those powers now or hereafter conferred by law.

A. Power to Invest. To invest and reinvest the Trust Estate in every kind of property, real, personal or mixed, and every kind of investment, specifically including but not by way of limitation, corporate obligations of every kind, stocks, preferred or common, shares of investment trusts, investment companies, mutual funds, market index funds and mortgage participations which individuals of prudence, discretion and intelligence acquire for their own account, and any common trust fund administered by any Trustee under this Trust Declaration.

B. Power to Retain Property. To retain any property which was an asset of the Trust Estate during the Settlor's lifetime or received without consideration by the Trustee as long as the Trustee deems advisable whether or not of the character permitted by law for the investment of trust funds. The trust properties and investment need not be diversified and the Trustee shall have no duty to dispose or convert any trust assets to effect diversification.

C. Power to Manage Securities. With respect to securities held in this Trust Declaration, to have all the rights, powers and privileges of an owner, including but not by way of limitation, the power to vote, give proxies and pay assessments, to participate in voting trusts, pooling agreements, foreclosures, reorganizations, consolidations, mergers, liquidations, sales and leases and, incident to such participation, to deposit securities with and transfer title to any protective or other committee on such terms as the Trustee may deem advisable, to exercise and sell stock subscription or conversion rights and to hold securities in "street name."

D. Power of Sale, Exchange, Repair. To manage, control, foreclose, repossess, grant options on, grant easements on, sell (for cash), convey, exchange, partition, divide, improve and repair trust property.

The power to sell, at the termination of the trust, any trust property if the Trustee feels said disposition would assist in the distribution of the trust property at termination.

E. Power to Lease. To lease trust property for terms within or beyond the term of the trust and for any purpose, including exploration for and removal of gas, oil and other minerals; and to enter into community oil leases, pooling and unitization agreements, operating agreements or otherwise, and to create restrictions, easements or other servitudes thereon, to assign, partition, divide, subdivide, transfer to a corporation in exchange for stock, improve, repair, loan, reloan, invest and reinvest the trust estate or any part thereof.

F. Power to Insure. To carry, at the expense of the Trust Estate, insurance of such kinds and in such amounts as the Trustee shall deem advisable to protect the Trust Estate and the Trustee against any hazard.

G. Power to Commence or Defend Litigation. To commence or defend such litigation with respect to the Trust or any property of the Trust Estate as the Trustee may deem advisable, at the expense of the Trust Declaration.

H. Power to Compromise Claim. To compromise or otherwise adjust any claims or litigation against or in favor of the Trust Declaration.

I. Power to Employ Consultants. To employ any custodian, investment advisor, attorney, accountant or other agents to assist the Trustee in administration of this Trust Declaration and to rely upon the advice given by these agents. Reasonable compensation shall be paid to these agents for all services performed.

J. Power to Adjust for Tax Consequences. To take any action and to make any election the Trustee shall deem advisable to minimize the tax liabilities of this trust and its beneficiaries, to allocate the benefits among the various beneficiaries and to make adjustments in the rights of any beneficiaries or group of beneficiaries or between principal and income accounts, to compensate for the consequences of any tax election or any investment decision or administrative decision that has the effect of preferring one beneficiary or group of beneficiaries over others, provided such discretion shall not be exercised in any manner which will cause a loss of or a decrease in any marital or charitable deduction otherwise allowable in computing the Settlor's federal estate tax.

ARTICLE V
MISCELLANEOUS

Paragraph 5.01. No Assignment. Each beneficiary hereunder is hereby prohibited from anticipating, encumbering, assigning or in any other manner, alienating her or his interest in either income or principal of any trust created under this Trust Declaration and is without power to do so nor shall such interest be subject to her or his liabilities or obligations nor to attachment, execution or other legal processes, bankruptcy proceedings or claims of creditors or others. The Trustee may require the personal receipt of a beneficiary as a condition precedent to payment, distribution or delivery of any amount, property or benefit hereunder. The Trustee may, however, deposit in any bank designated in writing, by a beneficiary, to her or his credit, income or principal payable to such beneficiary.

Paragraph 5.02. Principal and Income. Except as otherwise specifically provided in this Trust Declaration, the determination of all matters with respect to what shall constitute principal and income of each trust estate, gross income therefrom and net income distributable under the terms of the Trust Declaration, shall be governed by the provisions of the Revised Uniform Principal and Income Act as enacted in the State of (2a) Massachusetts , from time to time existing. All taxes, assessments, fees, charges and other expenses incurred by the Trustee in the administration, protection and distribution of each trust, shall be a charge upon the trust estate and shall be paid out of the income and/or principal, in accordance with the aforesaid Act.

Paragraph 5.03. Savings Clause. Unless sooner terminated in accordance with other provisions of this Trust Declaration, any trust created hereunder shall terminate twenty-one (21) years after the death of the last surviving member of the group consisting of the Settlor and the issue of the Settlor who are living and in being at the date of death of the Settlor.

Paragraph 5.04. Payments to Minors and Incompetents. The Trustee, in the Trustee's discretion, may apply payments directly for the benefit of any beneficiary, rather than directly to such beneficiary and, in the case of a beneficiary who is a minor or who is under any other disability, make payment to the guardian, conservator of the person or estate of such beneficiary, custodian under the Uniform Transfers to Minors Act, parent or any other suitable adult with whom the beneficiary resides or by expending the same for the care, education, maintenance or other benefit of said beneficiary. In addition, the Trustee, in the Trustee's discretion, may make payments directly to a beneficiary who is a minor if, in the Trustee's judgment, the minor is of sufficient age and maturity to properly manage the money or property so paid. The Trustee shall not be required to see to the application of any such payment so made to any said persons, but his, her or their receipt therefor shall be a full discharge to the Trustee.

Paragraph 5.05. No Physical Segregation. There need be no physical segregation or division of the various trusts except as segregation or division may be required by the termination of any of the trusts or as specifically provided, but the Trustee shall keep separate accounts for the different undivided interests.

Paragraph 5.06. Distribution. In any case in which the Trustee is required, pursuant to the provisions of the Trust, to divide any parts or shares for the purposes of distribution or otherwise, except as the donee of any power of appointment affecting such property may have expressly provided otherwise in the instrument exercising such power, the Trustee is authorized, in the Trustee's absolute discretion, to make the division and distribution (pro rata or otherwise) in kind, including an undivided interest in any property or partly in kind and partly in money, and for this purpose, to make such sales of the trust property as the Trustee may deem necessary, on such terms and conditions as the Trustee shall see fit. Any asset which is encumbered shall be assigned subject thereto, and its value or amount shall be given effect less such indebtedness.

Paragraph 5.07. Non-Pro Rata Distributions. As to distribution or division of property in kind under and for the several trusts, excepting the initial establishment of any trust for a pecuniary amount, the Trustee shall be cognizant of the differences between the tax cost bases and current value and shall endeavor, insofar as is practicable to distribute or set aside to or for each beneficiary or distributee, assets or property carrying amount or portions of the total unrealized taxable gains or losses embodied in all the assets and properties involved commensurate with the share or portion of each beneficiary or distributee.

Paragraph 5.08. Distribution If All Beneficiaries Die Before Full Distribution. If at any time before full distribution of the Trust Estate, the Settlor is deceased and no disposition of the property is directed by this Trust Declaration, the Trust Estate or the portion of it not disposed of under the Trust Declaration, whichever the case may be, shall thereupon be distributed to the Settlor's heirs at law under the laws of intestate succession of the State of (2a) __Massachusetts__ then in effect for separate property not acquired from a predeceased spouse.

Paragraph 5.09. Additional Property. With consent of the Trustee, additional property may be added at any time from any source to any trust held under this Trust Declaration. No person dealing with the Trustee in any manner shall be under any obligation to see to the application of any money paid to the Trustee or to inquire into the validity, expediency or propriety of any act of the Trustee or into any of the provisions of any trust hereunder.

Paragraph 5.10. Fiduciary Capacity. All of the powers of the Trustee provided in this Trust Declaration shall be exercisable by the Trustee in the Trustee's fiduciary capacity and only in such capacity.

Paragraph 5.11. Corporate Office. No person shall, by reason of acting as Trustee, be in any way restricted or prohibited from holding office in any corporation in which any trust under this Trust Declaration holds securities or from receiving compensation from any such corporation for services performed as a director, officer or employee of such corporation or from purchasing, selling or otherwise dealing with the stock of any such corporation for the individual account of such Trustee or from voting the stock of any such corporation held by such trust, including voting those shares in favor of the Settlor or any other person.

Paragraph 5.12. Disclaimer of Powers. The Settlor may disclaim, release or restrict the scope of any power held in connection with any trust created under this Trust Declaration, including any administrative power, whether such power is expressly granted in this Trust Declaration or implied by law, by a written instrument specifying the power to be disclaimed, released or restricted and the nature of any such restriction. Any power disclaimed or released by the Settlor shall be extinguished except to the extent this Trust Declaration expressly provides that such power pass to another. This power shall be personal to the Settlor only and may not be exercised by any other person acting on behalf of the Settlor, including, but not limited to, any Trustee (other than the Settlor), Conservator, agent or guardian.

Paragraph 5.13. Notice. Unless the Trustee has received written notice of the occurrence of an event affecting the beneficial interest in any trust held under this Trust Declaration, the Trustee shall not be liable to any beneficiary of such trust for any distributions made or other actions taken by the Trustee in good faith as though such event had not occurred.

Paragraph 5.14. Invalidity of Any Provision. Should any provision of this Trust Declaration be or become invalid or unenforceable, the remaining provisions of this Trust Declaration shall be and continue to be fully effective.

Paragraph 5.15. Gender and Number. Except as provided otherwise herein, the masculine, feminine and neuter gender, and the singular or plural number, shall each be deemed to include the others whenever the context so indicates.

Paragraph 5.16. Law of Construction of Trust. This Trust Declaration, its validity, the construction of and all rights under the Trusts provided for in this Trust Declaration shall be governed by the laws of the State of (2a)_ Massachusetts_ .

Paragraph 5.17. No Contest. The Settlor has intentionally and with full knowledge omitted to provide for his/her issue, ancestors, relatives and heirs living at the time of his/her demise, except for such provisions as are made specifically herein.

If any person who is or claims under or through a beneficiary of this Trust, or if any person who would be entitled to share in the Settlor's estate if the Settlor died intestate, should in any manner whatsoever, directly or indirectly, attack, contest or seek to impair or invalidate in court any provision of the following:
   A. This Trust or any Amendment to this Trust;
   B. Any Will or Codicil to any Will executed by the Settlor;
   C. Any beneficiary designation executed by the Settlor with respect to any insurance policy, any "Totten trust" account, any joint tenancy or tenancy by the entirety, any "transfer on death" account or any pension plan, or conspire or cooperate with anyone attempting to do any of the actions or things aforesaid, then each such person and any devise, share or interest in the Trust or the Settlor's Estate otherwise given to each such person under this Trust or the Settlor's Estate to which each such person might be entitled by law, is hereby revoked and shall pass and be distributed as though each such person had predeceased the Settlor leaving no issue or heirs whatsoever.

Any and every individual who asserts, or conspires or cooperates with any person who asserts, any claim against this Trust or the Estate of the Settlor of this Trust based on:

D. "Quantum meruit" theory;

E. Common law marriage, Marvin v. Marvin, 18 Cal. 3d 660 (1976) type of agreement or similar theory;

F. Constructive trust theory; or,

G. Oral agreement or written agreement which is to be proved by parole evidence, claiming that Settlor agreed to gift or devise anything to such person or to pay such person or another for services rendered, regardless of whether a court may find that such agreement existed, then each such person is disinherited and any devise, share or interest in this Trust or the Settlor's Estate otherwise given to each such person under this Trust or the Settlor's Estate or to which each such person might be entitled by law, is hereby revoked and shall pass and be distributed as though each such person had predeceased the Settlor leaving no issue or heirs whatsoever.

The Trustee is specifically authorized to defend any such attack, contest, claim or other proceeding of any nature concerning this Trust or of any provision hereof, and to employ legal counsel therefor, all at the expense of the Trust.

Paragraph 5.18. Survival. If any person fails to survive the Settlor by thirty (30) days, for all purposes of this Trust Declaration the person shall be considered to have predeceased the Settlor.

Paragraph 5.19. All typed and handwritten "fill-ins" where directed above were made before the execution of this Declaration of Trust and are not initialed by the Settlor. All crossed through words and interlineations were made before the execution of this Trust and are initialed by the Settlor.

CERTIFICATION OF SETTLOR

I certify that:

A.   I have read the foregoing Trust Declaration;

B.   The foregoing Trust Declaration correctly states the terms and conditions under which the Trust Estate is to be held, managed, administered and disposed of by the Trustee;

C.   As the Settlor named in such Trust Declaration, I approve such Trust Declaration in all particulars; and,

D.   As the Trustee named in such Trust Declaration, I approve and accept the Trust provided for in such Declaration.

220

Dated: (40) *Stephen Brown*
_____

                   (1)___STEPHEN BROWN_____, Settlor

                   (54) *Stephen Brown*
_____

                   (49)___STEPHEN BROWN_____, Trustee

STATE OF   (2a)__MASSACHUSETTS_____)
) ss.
COUNTY OF (2)___BARNSTABLE_____)

On __November 1__, 20_07__ before me, the undersigned, a Notary Public in and for said county and state, personally appeared (1)__STEPHEN BROWN____, personally known to me (or proved to me on the basis of satisfactory evidence) to be the person(s) whose name(s) is/are subscribed to the within instrument and acknowledged that he/she/they executed the same in his/her/their authorized capacity(ies), and that by his/her/their signature(s) on the instrument the person(s), or the entity upon behalf of which the person(s) acted, executed the instrument.

WITNESS my hand and official seal.

                   _*Noel Tara Public*_____
                   Notary Public in and for said County and State

EXHIBIT A

Property Declared to be assets of the (1a)_____ BROWN _____
TRUST dated (48)_____ 11-1-07 _____:

(55)

1.   4359 Red Roof Road, Barnstable, MA
2.   New England Bank Account #678431
3.   800 shares, common, IBM
4.   All other personal property

INTER VIVOS TRUST

THE (1a) <u>Washington Family Trust</u>

The Settlors named below hereby declare as follows:

ARTICLE I
ESTABLISHMENT OF TRUST

Paragraph 1.01. Creation of Trust. This Trust Declaration has been entered into between (1) <u>George Washington</u> and (4) <u>Martha Washington</u> as Settlors and themselves as the Trustees. The Settlors, of (2) <u>Fairfax</u> County, (2a) <u>Virginia</u>, have transferred, or will transfer, to the Trustees of this Trust Declaration the property described in the attached Exhibit "A" which will constitute, together with any other property that may be added to this Trust Declaration, the Trust Estate of an express trust which shall be held, administered and distributed by the Trustee as provided in this Trust Declaration.

Paragraph 1.02. Trust Name. This Trust Declaration shall be known as the (1a) " <u>Washington Family</u> TRUST" dated (48) <u>February 22, 2008</u> .

Paragraph 1.03. Definitions. As used in this Trust Declaration:

   A. Husband: The term "Husband" shall mean (1) <u>George Washington</u>

   B. Wife: The term "Wife" shall mean (4) <u>Martha Washington</u> .

   C. Settlors: The term "Settlors" shall refer collectively to Husband and Wife.

   D. Deceased Settlor: The term "deceased Settlor" shall refer to the Settlor who is first to die. However, the term, "then deceased Settlor" shall refer to the Settlor then deceased and may thus refer to the otherwise surviving Settlor.

   E. Surviving Settlor: The term "surviving Settlor" shall refer to the Settlor who is last to die.

F. Trustee: The term "Trustee" or "Trustees" shall refer to whoever is serving as Trustee or Trustees under this Trust Declaration.

G. Trust Estate: The term "Trust Estate" shall refer to the property subject to this Trust Declaration.

Paragraph 1.04. Property to Retain Status. All property now or hereafter transferred to the Trustee which was community property, quasi-community property or separate property at the time of such transfer, shall remain, respectively, community property, quasi-community property or the separate property of the spouse or spouses transferring such property to the Trustee.

ARTICLE II
OPERATION OF TRUST DURING THE LIFE OF HUSBAND AND WIFE

Paragraph 2.01. Net Income. During the life of Husband and/or Wife, the Trustee shall pay to or apply for the benefit of both Husband and Wife, or the survivor thereof, in monthly or more frequent intervals, all of the net income of the community Trust Estate and shall pay to or apply for the benefit of the contributing spouse, in monthly or more frequent intervals, all of the net income of the separate property contributed or owned by that spouse.

Paragraph 2.02. Withdrawal of Principal. During the life of Husband and/or Wife, the Trustee shall also pay to or apply for the benefit of both Husband and Wife, or either, or the survivor thereof, so much of the community principal of the Trust Estate, up to the whole thereof, as both Husband and Wife shall direct, and shall, at the discretion of a spouse, pay to or apply for the benefit of that spouse so much of the principal of the Trust Estate, up to the whole thereof, as is that spouse's separate property.

Paragraph 2.03. Incapacity of Husband or Wife. If, at any time either Husband or Wife has become physically or mentally incapacitated so as to be unable to manage his or her affairs, whether or not a court of competent jurisdiction has declared him or her incompetent, mentally ill, or in need of a conservator, the Trustee shall pay to the non-incapacitated spouse or apply for the benefit of either spouse such amounts of the principal and/or income of the community estate as may be necessary, in the Trustee's discretion, for the care, maintenance and support of both spouses in accordance with their accustomed manner of living. The Trustee shall also pay to or apply for the benefit of the incapacitated spouse such amounts of income or principal of the separate property contributed by the incapacitated spouse as may be necessary, in the Trustee's discretion, for the care, maintenance, and support of the incapacitated spouse in accordance with his or her accustomed manner of living, taking into account payments made by the Trustee from the community Trust Estate. If a conservator of the person or estate is appointed for the incapacitated spouse, the Trustee shall take into account any payments made for the incapacitated spouse's benefit by the conservator.

The payments specified in this Section shall be made until the incapacitated spouse is again able to manage his or her own affairs, or until the death of the first spouse to die, whichever event may occur earlier.

Paragraph 2.04. Revocation of Trust. At any time during their joint lives, either Husband or Wife as to community property, and either spouse as to his or her separate property, may, by serving written notice on the Trustee, revoke the Trust created by this Trust Declaration, in whole or in part. Any community property withdrawn from the Trust Estate by reason of any such revocation shall be delivered by the Trustee to both Husband and Wife and any separate property withdrawn from the Trust shall be delivered by the Trustee to the spouse revoking the Trust. After the death of the predeceasing Settlor, the surviving Settlor may, by serving written notice on the Trustee, revoke the trust created by this Declaration in whole or in part.

Paragraph 2.05. Amendment of Trust. At any time during their joint lives, Husband and Wife, jointly as to community property, and either spouse as to his or her separate property, may, by serving written notice on the Trustee, alter, modify or amend the Trust created by this Trust Declaration in any respect. After the death of the predeceasing Settlor the surviving Settlor may, by serving written notice on the Trustee, alter, modify or amend the Trust created by this Trust Declaration in any respect.

ARTICLE III
OPERATION OF TRUST AFTER DEATH OF DECEASED SETTLOR
AND DEATH OF SURVIVING SETTLOR

Paragraph 3.01. Collection of Assets and Payment of Debts: On the death of each Settlor the Trustee shall collect all assets belonging to the Trust Estate. As soon as practicable after the death of each Settlor the Trustee, except as otherwise provided herein, shall pay from the Trust Estate the just debts of the then deceased Settlor, as the case may be, (excluding any debts barred by provisions of law or not yet due), funeral expenses of the then deceased Settlor, and any inheritance, estate, or other death taxes that shall, by reason of the death of the then deceased Settlor, be attributable to the Trust Estate. This is not and shall not constitute a direction to pay all inheritance, estate or other death taxes from or charge the same to, the Trust Estate without apportionment.

Upon the death of the deceased Settlor all assets subject to this Declaration of Trust shall be and are confirmed as the separate property of the surviving Settlor.

Paragraph 3.02. Distribution of Trust Estate. Upon the death of the surviving Settlor, and after payment of expenses as set forth in Paragraph 3.01, the Trustee shall hold, administer and distribute the Trust Estate as follows:

A. The Trustee shall distribute to the following persons the cash amount listed after their respective names:

(10)   NOT APPLICABLE

B. The Trustee shall distribute to the following persons the real property described after their respective names. (12) Said real property is given free of all encumbrances or liens thereon.

(11) Robert Washington, the residence located at 1776 Mt.
      Vernon Dr., Mt. Vernon, VA
      end of list

C. The Trustee shall distribute to (13) **NOT APPLICABLE** a life estate in the following property located at: (14)_____. After the death of (13)_____ said property shall go, outright, to (15)_____ as the remainder person(s).

D. The Trustee shall distribute all of the rest, residue and remainder of the Trust Estate, real, personal and mixed, of whatsoever kind or character and wheresoever situated, to the following persons or entities (16) in the proportions listed after their names (17) in equal shares.

(18) Robert Washington, 100%
      end of list

E. Distribution of Trust Assets. With respect to the distribution of any trust estate upon termination of any trust, and partial distribution of any trust, the liquidation and distribution by the Trustee of the Trust Estate involved or the distributable portion shall commence immediately and be accomplished as rapidly as possible, and deliveries of the trust properties to the beneficiary or beneficiaries may be made in installments or series, retaining only reasonable reserves for final charges and expenses. In no event shall it be necessary for the Trustee to await an accounting to the Court, or any Court order, before releasing and distributing the majority of the Trust Estate to be distributed.

F. Undistributed Income. All the net income of the respective trusts or trust estates, not distributed, used or applied as otherwise provided herein, shall be accumulated and added to the principals of the respective trusts.

Upon the change or succession of any beneficiary, distribution of trust properties or any trust estate or any portion thereof, or upon setting aside, apportionment or division of any trust estate or upon the termination of a trust or any interest therein, the beneficial interest, properties or balance of trust estate at the applicable time and to be dealt with shall include any and all income accumulated, accrued, uncollected or held undistributed and all of such income shall likewise be distributed, set aside or apportioned to the next or succeeding beneficiaries, distributees, shares or trusts, retaining its character as income.

ARTICLE IV
TRUSTEES

Paragraph 4.01. Appointment of Trustees. Settlors, (1)___George Washington___ and (4)_Martha Washington_ are appointed and confirmed as the Trustees, without bond. In the event either original Trustee should resign, die or become mentally incapacitated, the remaining Trustee shall act as sole Trustee. If either original Trustee should cease to act as Trustee due to a mental incapacity, his/her restoration of mental capacity shall result in his immediate return as Trustee or Co-Trustee hereunder. If either original Trustee should cease to act as sole Trustee or a Co-Trustee with the other original Trustee due to his/her resignation, he/she may at any time subsequent, elect to act again as sole Trustee or a Co-Trustee with the other original Trustee. Said election shall be made by filing same with either of the then acting Trustee or by recording said election in the County of residence of said Trustee making such election.

In the event both (1)_George Washington_ and (4)_Martha Washington_ should die, refuse to act, or for any other reason be unable to act, then (25)_Thomas Jefferson_ shall act as (26)____Trustee hereunder (27) without bond. In the event he/she/they should die, decline to act, or for any other reason, be unable to act as Trustee then (28)____Benjamin Franklin____ shall act as Trustee hereunder (27) without bond.

Paragraph 4.02. Substitute Trustee. The Settlors jointly, or the surviving Settlor upon the death of the predeceased Settlor, may appoint a substitute or successor Trustee to act as Trustee of any trust or trusts created hereunder in the place and stead of, or as successor to, any Trustee named in Section 4.01 above. Such substitution shall be in writing.

Paragraph 4.03. Trustee Liability. No person named as Trustee in this instrument or appointed as Trustee in the manner specified herein shall be liable to any beneficiary or to any heir of either Settlor for the Trustee's acts or failure to act, except for willful misconduct or gross negligence. No such Trustee shall be liable or responsible for any act, omission or default of any other Trustee provided that they shall have had no knowledge of facts that might reasonably be expected to put the Trustee on notice of it.

Paragraph 4.04. Title to Trust Estate. The legal title to all property held in trust hereunder shall be, remain and become vested in the Trustee or successor Trustee from time to time acting hereunder, without any act of conveyance or transfer to or by or acceptance from, any succeeding, retiring or predecessor Trustee; however, any removed or resigning Trustee shall execute and deliver any and all conveyances and documents requested and reasonably necessary to transfer the trust estate and its assets to a successor Trustee. Each successor Trustee from time to time acting hereunder shall have all the rights, powers, immunities and authorities, discretionary or otherwise and the duties and obligations herein granted to the original Trustee. No successor Trustee shall be obligated to inquire into or be in any way responsible for the previous administration of any trust created herein or of the trust estate or for any act or default of any predecessor Trustee.

Paragraph 4.05. Powers of Trustee. To carry out the purposes of any trust created under this Trust Declaration, and subject to any limitations stated elsewhere in this Trust Declaration, the Trustee is vested with the following powers with respect to the Trust Estate, and any part of it, in addition to those powers now or hereafter conferred by law.

A. Power to Invest. To invest and reinvest the Trust Estate in every kind of property, real, personal or mixed, and every kind of investment, specifically including but not by way of limitation, corporate obligations of every kind, stocks, preferred or common, shares of investment trusts, investment companies, mutual funds, market index funds and mortgage participations which individuals of prudence, discretion and intelligence acquire for their own account, and any common trust fund administered by any Trustee under this Trust Declaration.

B. Power to Retain Property. To retain any property which was an asset of the Trust Estate during the Settlor's lifetime or received without consideration by the Trustee as long as the Trustee deems advisable whether or not of the character permitted by law for the investment of trust funds. The trust properties and investment need not be diversified and the Trustee shall have no duty to dispose or convert any trust assets to effect diversification.

C. Power to Manage Securities. With respect to securities held in this Trust Declaration, to have all the rights, powers and privileges of an owner, including but not by way of limitation, the power to vote, give proxies and pay assessments, to participate in voting trusts, pooling agreements, foreclosures, reorganizations, consolidations, mergers, liquidations, sales and leases and, incident to such participation, to deposit securities with and transfer title to any protective or other committee on such terms as the Trustee may deem advisable, to exercise and sell stock subscription or conversion rights and to hold securities in "street name."

D. Power of Sale, Exchange, Repair. To manage, control, foreclose, repossess, grant options on, grant easements on, sell (for cash), convey, exchange, partition, divide, improve and repair trust property.

The power to sell, at the termination of the trust, any trust property if the Trustee feels said disposition would assist in the distribution of the trust property at termination.

E. Power to Lease. To lease trust property for terms within or beyond the term of the trust and for any purpose, including exploration for and removal of gas, oil and other minerals; and to enter into community oil leases, pooling and unitization agreements, operating agreements or otherwise, and to create restrictions, easements or other servitudes thereon, to assign, partition, divide, subdivide, transfer to a corporation in exchange for stock, improve, repair, loan, reloan, invest and reinvest the trust estate or any part thereof.

F. Power to Insure. To carry, at the expense of the Trust Estate, insurance of such kinds and in such amounts as the Trustee shall deem advisable to protect the Trust Estate and the Trustee against any hazard.

G. Power to Commence or Defend Litigation. To commence or defend such litigation with respect to the Trust or any property of the Trust Estate as the Trustee may deem advisable, at the expense of the Trust Declaration.

H. Power to Compromise Claim. To compromise or otherwise adjust any claims or litigation against or in favor of the Trust Declaration.

I. Power to Employ Consultants. To employ any custodian, investment advisor, attorney, accountant or other agents to assist the Trustee in administration of this Trust Declaration and to rely upon the advice given by these agents. Reasonable compensation shall be paid to these agents for all services performed.

J. Power to Adjust for Tax Consequences. To take any action and to make any election the Trustee shall deem advisable to minimize the tax liabilities of this trust and its beneficiaries, to allocate the benefits among the various beneficiaries and to make adjustments in the rights of any beneficiaries or group of beneficiaries or between principal and income accounts, to compensate for the consequences of any tax election or any investment decision or administrative decision that has the effect of preferring one beneficiary or group of beneficiaries over others, provided such discretion shall not be exercised in any manner which will cause a loss of or a decrease in any marital or charitable deduction otherwise allowable in computing the then deceased Settlor's federal estate tax.

K. Trust Bank and Securities Accounts. During the joint lives of the Settlors, if the Settlors are serving as co-Trustees hereunder, the signature of either Trustor shall be sufficient to create, negotiate or endorse trust checks or to deposit or withdraw trust funds from trust bank or securities accounts or to trade securities in said securities accounts.

ARTICLE V
MISCELLANEOUS

Paragraph 5.01. No Assignment. Each beneficiary hereunder is hereby prohibited from anticipating, encumbering, assigning or in any other manner, alienating her or his interest in either income or principal of any trust created under this Trust Declaration and is without power to do so nor shall such interest be subject to her or his liabilities or obligations nor to attachment, execution or other legal processes, bankruptcy proceedings or claims of creditors or others. The Trustee may require the personal receipt of a beneficiary as a condition precedent to payment, distribution or delivery of any amount, property or benefit hereunder. The Trustee may, however, deposit in any bank designated in writing, by a beneficiary, to her or his credit, income or principal payable to such beneficiary.

Paragraph 5.02. Principal and Income. Except as otherwise specifically provided in this Trust Declaration, the determination of all matters with respect to what shall constitute principal and income of each trust estate, gross income therefrom and net income distributable under the terms of the Trust Declaration, shall be governed by the provisions of the Revised Uniform Principal and Income Act as enacted in the State of (2a)_____Virginia_____, from time to time existing. All taxes, assessments, fees, charges and other expenses incurred by the Trustee in the administration, protection and distribution of each trust, shall be a charge upon the trust estate and shall be paid out of the income and/or principal, in accordance with the aforesaid Act.

Paragraph 5.03. Savings Clause. Unless sooner terminated in accordance with other provisions of this Trust Declaration, any trust created hereunder shall terminate twenty-one (21) years after the death of the last surviving member of the group consisting of the Settlor and the issue of the Settlor who are living and in being at the date of death of the Settlor.

Paragraph 5.04. Payments to Minors and Incompetents. The Trustee, in the Trustee's discretion, may apply payments directly for the benefit of any beneficiary, rather than directly to such beneficiary and, in the case of a beneficiary who is a minor or who is under any other disability, make payment to the guardian, conservator of the person or estate of such beneficiary, custodian under the Uniform Transfers to Minors Act, parent or any other suitable adult with whom the beneficiary resides or by expending the same for the care, education, maintenance or other benefit of said beneficiary. In addition, the Trustee, in the Trustee's discretion, may make payments directly to a beneficiary who is a minor if, in the Trustee's judgment, the minor is of sufficient age and maturity to properly manage the money or property so paid. The Trustee shall not be required to see to the application of any such payment so made to any said persons, but his, her or their receipt therefor shall be a full discharge to the Trustee.

Paragraph 5.05. No Physical Segregation. There need be no physical segregation or division of the various trusts except as segregation or division may be required by the termination of any of the trusts or as specifically provided, but the Trustee shall keep separate accounts for the different undivided interests.

Paragraph 5.06. Distribution. In any case in which the Trustee is required, pursuant to the provisions of the Trust, to divide any parts or shares for the purposes of distribution or otherwise, except as the donee of any power of appointment affecting such property may have expressly provided otherwise in the instrument exercising such power, the Trustee is authorized, in the Trustee's absolute discretion, to make the division and distribution (pro rata or otherwise) in kind, including an undivided interest in any property or partly in kind and partly in money, and for this purpose, to make such sales of the trust property as the Trustee may deem necessary, on such terms and conditions as the Trustee shall see fit. Any asset which is encumbered shall be assigned subject thereto, and its value or amount shall be given effect less such indebtedness.

Paragraph 5.07. Non-Pro Rata Distributions. As to distribution or division of property in kind under and for the several trusts, excepting the initial establishment of any trust for a pecuniary amount, the Trustee shall be cognizant of the differences between the tax cost bases and current value and shall endeavor, insofar as is practicable to distribute or set aside to or for each beneficiary or distributee, assets or property carrying amount or portions of the total unrealized taxable gains or losses embodied in all the assets and properties involved commensurate with the share or portion of each beneficiary or distributee.

Paragraph 5.08. Distribution If All Beneficiaries Die Before Full Distribution. If at any time before full distribution of the Trust Estate, the Settlor is deceased and no disposition of the property is directed by this Trust Declaration, the Trust Estate or the portion of it not disposed of under the Trust Declaration, whichever the case may be, shall thereupon be distributed one-half to those persons who would be the legal heirs of Husband and one-half to the legal heirs of Wife their identities and respective shares to be determined as though the death of Husband and Wife had occurred immediately following the event requiring distribution and according to the laws of the State of (2a)___**Virginia**___ then in effect relating to the succession of separate property not acquired from a parent, grandparent or previously deceased spouse.

Paragraph 5.09. Additional Property. With consent of the Trustee, additional property may be added at any time from any source to any trust held under this Trust Declaration. No person dealing with the Trustee in any manner shall be under any obligation to see to the application of any money paid to the Trustee or to inquire into the validity, expediency or propriety of any act of the Trustee or into any of the provisions of any trust hereunder.

Paragraph 5.10. Fiduciary Capacity. All of the powers of the Trustee provided in this Trust Declaration shall be exercisable by the Trustee in the Trustee's fiduciary capacity and only in such capacity.

Paragraph 5.11. Corporate Office. No person shall, by reason of acting as Trustee, be in any way restricted or prohibited from holding office in any corporation in which any trust under this Trust Declaration holds securities or from receiving compensation from any such corporation for services performed as a director, officer or employee of such corporation or from purchasing, selling or otherwise dealing with the stock of any such corporation for the individual account of such Trustee or from voting the stock of any such corporation held by such trust, including voting those shares in favor of the Settlor or any other person.

Paragraph 5.12. Disclaimer of Powers. The Trustee may disclaim, release or restrict the scope of any power held in connection with any trust created under this Trust Declaration, including any administrative power, whether such power is expressly granted in this Trust Declaration or implied by law, by a written instrument specifying the power to be disclaimed, released or restricted and the nature of any such restriction. Any power disclaimed or released by the Trustee shall be extinguished except to the extent this Trust Declaration expressly provides that such power pass to another. This power shall be personal to the Trustee only and may not be exercised by any other person acting on behalf of the Trustee, including, but not limited to, any Trustee (other than the Trustee), Conservator, agent or guardian.

Paragraph 5.13. Notice. Unless the Trustee has received written notice of the occurrence of an event affecting the beneficial interest in any trust held under this Trust Declaration, the Trustee shall not be liable to any beneficiary of such trust for any distributions made or other actions taken by the Trustee in good faith as though such event had not occurred.

Paragraph 5.14. Invalidity of Any Provision. Should any provision of this Trust Declaration be or become invalid or unenforceable, the remaining provisions of this Trust Declaration shall be and continue to be fully effective.

Paragraph 5.15. Gender and Number. Except as provided otherwise herein, the masculine, feminine and neuter gender, and the singular or plural number, shall each be deemed to include the others whenever the context so indicates.

Paragraph 5.16. Law of Construction of Trust. This Trust Declaration, its validity, the construction of and all rights under the Trusts provided for in this Trust Declaration shall be governed by the laws of the State of (2a)_____Virginia_____.

Paragraph 5.17. No Contest. The Settlors have intentionally and with full knowledge omitted to provide for his/her issue, ancestors, relatives and heirs living at the time of his/her demise, except for such provisions as are made specifically herein.

If any person who is or claims under or through a beneficiary of this Trust, or if any person who would be entitled to share in either Settlor's estate if either or both Settlors died intestate, should in any manner whatsoever, directly or indirectly, attack, contest or seek to impair or invalidate in court any provision of the following:

A. This Trust or any Amendment to this Trust;

B. Any Will or Codicil to any Will executed by either Settlor;

C. Any beneficiary designation executed by either Settlor with respect to any insurance policy, any "Totten trust" account, any joint tenancy or tenancy by the entirety, any "transfer on death" account or any pension plan, or conspire or cooperate with anyone attempting to do any of the actions or things aforesaid, then each such person and any devise, share or interest in the Trust or either Settlor's Estate otherwise given to each such person under this Trust or either Settlor's Estate to which each such person might be entitled by law, is hereby revoked and shall pass and be distributed as though each such person had predeceased either Settlor leaving no issue or heirs whatsoever.

Any and every individual who asserts, or conspires or cooperates with any person who asserts, any claim against this Trust or the Estate of either Settlor of this Trust based on.

D. "Quantum meruit" theory;

E. Common law marriage, Marvin v. Marvin, 18 Cal. 3d 660 (1976) type of agreement or similar theory;

F. Constructive trust theory; or,

G. Oral agreement or written agreement which is to be proved by parole evidence, claiming that either Settlor agreed to gift or devise anything to such person or to pay such person or another for services rendered, regardless of whether a court may find that such agreement existed, then each such person is disinherited and any devise, share or interest in this Trust or either Settlor's Estate otherwise given to each such person under this Trust or either Settlor's Estate or to which each such person might be entitled by law, is hereby revoked and shall pass and be distributed as though each such person had predeceased both Settlors leaving no issue or heirs whatsoever.

The Trustee is specifically authorized to defend any such attack, contest, claim or other proceeding of any nature concerning this Trust or of any provision hereof, and to employ legal counsel therefor, all at the expense of the Trust.

Paragraph 5.18. Survival. If any person fails to survive a Settlor by thirty (30) days, for all purposes of this Trust Declaration the person shall be considered to have predeceased such Settlor.

Paragraph 5.19. All typed and handwritten "fill-ins" where directed above were made before the execution of this Declaration of Trust and are not initialed by the Settlors. All crossed through words and interlineations were made before the execution of this Trust and are initialed by the Settlors.

CERTIFICATION OF HUSBAND AND WIFE

We, and each of us, certify that:

A. We, and each of us, have read the foregoing Trust Declaration;

B. The foregoing Trust Declaration correctly states the terms and conditions under which the Trust Estate is to be held, managed, administered and disposed of by the Trustee;

C. As the Settlors named in such Trust Declaration, we, and each of us, approve such Trust Declaration in all particulars; and

D. As the Trustees named in such Trust Declaration, we, and each of us, approve and accept the Trust provided for in such Declaration.

Dated: (40)_*George Washington*_____

               (1)___George Washington_____, Settlor, Trustee

               (1b)_*Martha Washington*_____

               (4)____Martha Washington_____, Settlor, Trustee

STATE OF   (2a)_____Virginia_____)
) ss.
COUNTY OF   (2)_____Fairfax_____)

On __February 22___, 20_08_ before me, the undersigned, a Notary Public in and for said county and state, personally appeared (1)_George Washington_ and (4)_Martha Washington_, personally known to me (or proved to me on the basis of satisfactory evidence) to be the person(s) whose name(s) is/are subscribed to the within instrument and acknowledged that he/she/they executed the same in his/her/their authorized capacity(ies), and that by his/her/their signature(s) on the instrument the person(s), or the entity upon behalf of which the person(s) acted, executed the instrument.

WITNESS my hand and official seal.

Noel Tara Public
_____
Notary Public in and for said County and State

EXHIBIT A

Property Declared to be assets of the (1a)___**Washington Family**___ TRUST
dated (48)___**2-22-08**___:

(55)

1. The residence located at 1776 Mt. Vernon Dr., Mt. Vernon, VA
2. All livestock owned by the Settlors
3. All Revolutionary War Memorabilia owned by the Settlors
4. Presidential Stamp Collection owned by the Settlors

AMENDMENT TO THE (1A) JOHNSON TRUST

THE (1a)_____JOHNSON_____ TRUST was created (48)___8-28-07___, by Declaration of Trust of (1)Nicholas Johnson, in his/her capacity as Settlor with (56) Nicholas Johnson in his/her/their capacity as Trustee(s). Said Trust has (57) not been previously amended.

In accordance with the enabling provisions of the Trust instrument, THE (1a)_ JOHNSON _ TRUST dated (48)___8-28-07___, is (58) further amended and modified as hereinafter set forth.

1. Article __IV__ , Section ___4.01___ is hereby amended to read in full as follows:

Paragraph 4.01. Appointment of Trustees. (49)__Nicholas Johnson__ is appointed and confirmed as the Trustee(s). In the event (49) Nicholas Johnson should die, refuse to act, or for any other reason be unable to act as Trustee then (25)_____Lisa Johnson_____ shall act as (26)____Trustee hereunder (27) without bond. In the event he/she/they should die, decline to act, or for any other reason, be unable to act as Trustee then (28)_____Joseph Johnson_____ shall act as Trustee hereunder (27) without bond.

CERTIFICATION OF SETTLOR and TRUSTEE

I, (1)__Nicholas Johnson__ , certify that:

A. I have read the foregoing amendment to my Declaration of Trust;

B. The foregoing amendment to my Declaration of Trust correctly states the terms and conditions under which the Trust is to be held, managed, administered, and disposed of by the Trustee; and,

C. As the Settlor approve such Declaration of Trust, as amended herein, in all particulars.

I, (1)____Nicholas Johnson_____, certify that:

As Trustee I approve and accept such Declaration of Trust, as amended herein, in all particulars.

STATE OF   (2a)____Iowa_____)
) ss.
COUNTY OF (2)_____Benton_____)

On ____10-1_____, 20_09_ before me, the undersigned, a Notary Public in and for said county and state, personally appeared (1)__Nicholas Johnson___, personally known to me (or proved to me on the basis of satisfactory evidence) to be the person(s) whose name(s) is/are subscribed to the within instrument and acknowledged that he/she/they executed the same in his/her/their authorized capacity(ies), and that by his/her/their signature(s) on the instrument the person(s), or the entity upon behalf of which the person(s) acted, executed the instrument.

WITNESS my hand and official seal.

_____*Noel Tara Public*_____
Notary Public in and for said County and State

TRUST CERTIFICATION

1. EXISTENCE OF TRUST AND DATE OF EXECUTION: The (1a)___Washington Family___ TRUST created (48) February 22 2008 is in existence and was executed on (48)___February 22 2008___

2. IDENTITY OF SETTLORS: (1)___George Washington___ and (4)___Martha Washington___

3. IDENTITY OF CURRENTLY ACTING TRUSTEE(S): (49)___George Washington___

4. IDENTITY OF SUCCESSOR TRUSTEE(S): In the event (49)___George Washington___ should decline, become unable or, for any reason, cease to serve as a Trustee then (51)___Martha Washington___ shall act as Trustee(s).

5. REVOCABILITY OF TRUST: Said Trust is revocable and said power is held by the Settlors.

6. TRUST TAX IDENTIFICATION NUMBER: The trust uses the Social Security number of either of the Settlors:

7. TITLE TO TRUST ASSETS: Title to trust assets should be (49) "___George Washington___, Trustee of the (1a)___Washington Family___ Trust dated (48)___February 22 2008___."

8. MATERIAL AMENDMENT OR REVOCATION OF TRUST: Said Trust has not been amended or revoked in any manner which would cause a representation made herein to be incorrect.

9. POWERS OF THE TRUSTEES: To carry out the purposes of any trust created under this Declaration of Trust, and subject to any limitations stated elsewhere in

this Declaration, the Trustee is vested with the following powers with respect to the Trust Estate, and any part of it, in addition to those powers now or hereafter conferred by law.

See Attached Powers

(Paragraph 4.5 or Paragraph 4.6)

(53)Paragraph 4.05. Powers of Trustee. To carry out the purposes of any trust created under this Trust Declaration, and subject to any limitations stated elsewhere in this Trust Declaration, the Trustee is vested with the following powers with respect to the Trust Estate, and any part of it, in addition to those powers now or hereafter conferred by law.

CERTIFICATION OF TRUSTEE(S)

I, certify that I have read the foregoing Trust Certification and that the foregoing Trust Certification is correct as to matters stated therein.

STATE OF   (2a)___**Virginia**___)

) ss.

COUNTY OF   (2)___**Fairfax**___)

On ___**July 4**___ , 20_**09**_ before me, the undersigned, a Notary Public in and for said county and state, personally appeared (49)___**George Washington**___, personally known to me (or proved to me on the basis of satisfactory evidence) to be the person(s) whose name(s) is/are subscribed to the within instrument and acknowledged that he/she/they executed the same in his/her/their authorized capacity(ies), and that by his/her/their signature(s) on the instrument the person(s), or the entity upon behalf of which the person(s) acted, executed the instrument.

WITNESS my hand and official seal.

Noel Tara Public
_____
Notary Public in and for said County and State

REVOCATION OF THE (1A) Ralph Reed TRUST

Recitals: The (1a) **Ralph Reed** TRUST was created (48) **April 22, 2008** , by Declaration of Trust by (1) **Ralph Reed** in his or her capacity as Settlor with himself/herself in his or her capacity as Trustee. Said Settlor now wishes to revoke said Trust in full.

REVOCATION: In accordance with the enabling provisions of the trust instrument, the (1a) **Ralph Reed Trust** , is hereby revoked in full.

IN WITNESS WHEREOF, the Settlor has duly executed this Revocation of the (1a) **Ralph Reed Trust** and made the same fully effective this date.

Dated:
(40) *Ralph Reed*

(1) **Ralph Reed** , Settlor

STATE OF (2a) **DuPage**)
) ss.
COUNTY OF (2) **Illinois**)

On ___October 20___, 20_10_ before me, the undersigned, a Notary Public in and for said county and state, personally appeared (1)_Ralph Reed_____ personally known to me (or proved to me on the basis of satisfactory evidence) to be the person(s) whose name(s) is/are subscribed to the within instrument and acknowledged that he/she/they executed the same in his/her/their authorized capacity(ies), and that by his/her/their signature(s) on the instrument the person(s), or the entity upon behalf of which the person(s) acted, executed the instrument.

WITNESS my hand and official seal.

_____*Noel Tara Public*_____
Notary Public in and for said County and State

ASSIGNMENT

The undersigned, (1)___George Washington___, owner of the (complete description of asset):

   500 cases of Lafayette 1776 port wine

hereby Assigns same to (49)___George Washington___ and (if applicable) (58)_____Martha Washington_____ Trustee(s) of the (1a)___Washington Family Trust___ dated (48) February 22, 2008 .
The undersigned, as Trustee(s) of said Trust hereby accepts said Assignment.

Date:

(40)___*George Washington*___

(1)___George Washington___

(1b)___*Martha Washington*___

(4)___Martha Washington___

(Optional)

STATE OF _____Virginia_____)
) ss.
COUNTY OF _____Mt. Vernon_____)

On <u>March 3</u> , 20<u>08</u> before me, the undersigned, a Notary Public in and for said county and state, personally appeared (1)<u>George Washington</u> and (4)<u>Martha Washington</u> , personally known to me (or proved to me on the basis of satisfactory evidence) to be the person(s) whose name(s) is/are subscribed to the within instrument and acknowledged that he/she/they executed the same in his/her/their authorized capacity(ies), and that by his/her/their signature(s) on the instrument the person(s), or the entity upon behalf of which the person(s) acted, executed the instrument.

WITNESS my hand and official seal.

Nancy Notary
Notary Public in and for said County and State

Index

About the Author

Douglas E. Godbe has practiced law in California for over twenty years. He is a California State Bar Certified specialist in probate, estate planning, and trust law. Mr. Godbe's offices are in Laguna Hills, California.